ABOUT THE BOOK

D1063410

"This is the best, direct, understandable book on prayer I have come across. It is so simple that those who really desire to know how to pray can, by easy steps, learn. The author is most definite and most positive as step by step she leads the reader or student into prayer faith and a realization that prayer is *conversation* with God and that *we must* await His reply. The several helps for personal and group aids in prayer sum it all up 'perfectly.'"

—MRS. GEORGE DAVIS for the
Southern Baptist Sunday School Board

ABOUT THE AUTHOR

Rosalind Rinker has served the Lord in many ways. She was a writer-missionary in China for twelve years, working with the Oriental Missionary Society and Mrs. Charles E. Cowman. After returning to the United States, she spent three years speaking in churches across the country, after which she served twelve years with Inter-Varsity Christian Fellowship in New York City and the Pacific Coast areas. She now travels extensively speaking on prayer and related subjects.

PRAYER

Conversing with God

ROSALIND RINKER

Zondervan Books • Grand Rapids, Michigan

To
My Mother
who led me to Christ

PRAYER — CONVERSING WITH GOD
Copyright © 1959 by Zondervan Publishing House
All rights reserved

First printing Zondervan Books edition March 1968
Second printing July 1968
Third printing January 1969
Fourth printing August 1969
Fifth printing March 1970
Sixth printing August 1970
Seventh printing February 1971
Eighth printing August 1971
Ninth printing December 1971

ZONDERVAN BOOKS are published by Zondervan Publishing
House, 1415 Lake Drive, S.E., Grand Rapids, Mich. 49506,
U.S.A.

Printed in the United States of America

PREFACE

I HAVE DISCOVERED THAT PRAYER'S REAL PURPOSE IS TO put God at the center of our attention, and forget ourselves and the impression we are making on others.

The content of this book is largely autobiographical, because there was no other way to describe the intimate experiences through which God took me in learning the true meaning of prayer.

The title might have been, *Matthew* 18:19, 20 or *When Two or Three Agree*, for the book is based largely on the meaning and contents of those verses. Through a period of more than twenty-five years of my Christian life, I fought the various hindrances to prayer and finally discovered that in the very things that bothered me, lay the key to the new and wonderful lessons God had for me. As I have shared these with various groups, I have seen others find the simplicity of conversational prayer transform and light up the meaning of prayer. One group which spent most of the time singing and giving requests and only about five minutes in prayer, reversed the process and began to pray conversationally. With joyful astonishment they found they wanted to spend a whole hour praying together!

Group prayer has lost its meaning for many of us, so that any excuse is a good excuse for not going to a prayer meeting. Praying conversationally (that is, praying back and forth on a single subject until a new one is introduced by the Spirit) makes prayer such a natural means of "spiritual togetherness" that the healing love of God touches us all as we are in His presence. Meeting the Lord in this way brings us to the anticipated realization of what it means to be consciously with Him, and to belong to one another as brothers and sisters in Christ.

I would like to express my deep appreciation to all those who have encouraged and helped me continue my search for reality in prayer. To the missionaries with whom I worked in China, to the Staff and students of Inter-Varsity Christian Fellowship in America; to the Rev. Mr. Harold De Vries, Winnetka Bible Church, Winnetka, Illinois, Rev. Mr. George Wingard, First Methodist Church, Otsego,

Michigan, Rev. Mr. Paris Reidhead, Gospel Tabernacle, New York City, the directors and participants of Mound Keswick, Cedar Lake and Cannon Beach Bible Conferences, for the privilege of actually testing the material in this book, my heartfelt thanks.

For her daily sharing with me in prayer and for her encouragement and help with the manuscript, I am deeply grateful to Eugenia Price, with whom I am associated in the great adventure with God.

ROSALIND RINKER

Chicago, Illinois
August, 1959

CONTENTS

CHAPTER 1

THREE PRAYER MEETINGS

The first one

For the first fifteen years of my Christian life, I played follow-the-leader where prayer was concerned. In my desire to be a true disciple of Jesus Christ, I somehow found myself following others instead of following Him.

My Christian life began when I was a sophomore in high school. Mother took me to a youth conference where I gave my heart and my life to Jesus Christ. In the next chapter I shall tell you some of what happened when I unconsciously began imitating other Christians. But before I began following people there was one shining moment about which I want to tell you.

On a snowy North Dakota night, I had a difficult choice to make for a girl of fifteen. In the little town where I was born, there was a party at one house and a cottage prayer meeting at another on the same night. I chose the cottage prayer meeting.

The little brown frame house was packed with people. I looked around, as teenagers do, and couldn't spot a single person my age. My first thought was to get out, but the house was too small and too crowded. Anyway, hadn't I already made my choice? And God knew, didn't He, when I asked Him where to go that Friday night, that there wouldn't be anyone my age at the meeting?

I stayed. There was a Bible reading. Then everyone knelt. So did I. Sometimes I felt I was only an onlooker. How did they know when to pray? Who told them? My heart beat faster. Should I pray, too? Where, I asked myself, did *that* idea come from? Me pray aloud? In front of all those people? When I was the only teenager present? Probably no one even knew I was there.

Faster and faster went my heart. The person who had been praying for some time stopped. There was silence. No. No. No! I couldn't break it! Let someone else do it.

Cautiously I asked myself, who am I arguing with about this thing? Myself? Could it be that God was asking me to pray aloud in front of all these people? What difference could it make to God if I did or if I didn't?

While I was still struggling with my thoughts and my objections, an older lady began to pray. I sighed with temporary relief.

Why, I said to myself, she can't even speak English! No one can understand a word she is saying, and here she is praying where people can hear her. I listened some more. A sentence or two in German, then a smattering of English, then more German.

I withheld further judgment and listened again. Suddenly I felt my heart was being held in God's hand. The old German lady was crying! And she wasn't ashamed to be praying or crying. And the tenderness in her voice told me that her tears were not those of frustration, but of real love for her Lord. She was speaking *to Him. Not to us.* And He was there. I knew it. *He was there.*

The rapid conversation in my heart went on: And *you* can speak English and *you* belong to God in a new way since last June and are *you* still afraid? That was enough. I recognized the voice of Jesus, Lover that He is. I would pray aloud, and I would speak straight to Him. I would not be afraid and I would not care if there were tears, and I would not care if my words got tangled up and I would not care if my prayer was like the other or if it wasn't. I would forget all those people and just think about Him.

And I did. "Dear Lord Jesus ..." I heard myself praying aloud for the first time in my life. And I did cry and my words did get tangled, but it was all right. I had spoken to Him. He was there.

He had been there all the time I was arguing with myself. And He was there when I spoke to Him aloud with other people listening.

As the snow crunched under my feet that cold winter night on my way home, my heart was warm with the freshness of talking with Jesus Christ. I had met Him. I had had my first flash of insight about prayer.

Perhaps I understood as only the very young understand easily, that He meant it when He said,

*... where two or three
are gathered together in my
name, there am I
in the midst of them.*

The second one

After that first "shining moment" when I knew that prayer was talking person to person with the Lord Jesus, I was no longer afraid to pray aloud. He loved me and I loved Him, and all the world was new, and I was young and life was good. I wanted to be the best kind of Christian there was. I wanted to learn how to pray in the right way, and began to keep my ears open to see how other people prayed and what they said and how they said it.

Since I was no longer afraid to pray in public, it was easy to pick up pointers and to begin to use them. Several things impressed me right away: The language people used, and the way they addressed God. I also noticed that when the pastor's wife prayed, people said "Amen" and "Yes, Lord." When she said the right thing they seemed to be encouraged and agreed with her and said so. It bothered me for a while, but soon I found myself praying like Mrs. O. and wanting to say things that would make people say "Amen" to my prayers, too.

Apparently, the tone of voice was something to watch, if one wanted to be really fervent in prayer. An unconsciously dramatic tone which was different and pitched higher than the usual conversation voice seemed preferable. This tone kept climbing and climbing until it reached a climax of some kind, and then came down and started again. It sounded like a good way to persuade God that one meant business.

God knows I was in dead earnest over the whole matter. I think I got rather restless sometimes, but wouldn't have admitted it to anyone for the world. The first inkling I had of this restlessness was once when I heard a dear sister in the church pray. She climbed the heights and prayed around the world. Suddenly I "heard" the tone of her voice, and thought to myself, if I didn't know who is praying, I wouldn't know it was Mrs. R. I wonder if God wants us to talk to Him in that unnatural tone of voice?

How can we be our real selves with Him if we pray like that?

I was shocked at myself for thinking such thoughts. But the idea persisted.

"How can God talk to you when you are praying, if you are shouting at Him like that? Why don't you give Him a chance to say a word?" I was a bit uneasy, I'll admit, trying to answer that one. But I put it carefully aside, because who was I to try to reform the prayer meeting? Besides, "being spiritual" was pretty important to me, because I was just at the age when being approved meant everything.

It was a glorious day when I was "approved" by a foreign missionary society and sent to China at the age of twenty as a secretary in the missionary office. I was deeply sincere in that I felt this was where God was guiding me to work for Him, and I tried with my whole heart to enter into all that pertained to the mission work.

On the field there was the regular Friday night staff prayer meeting. The entire evening was devoted to this meeting. We sang, had a message from the Bible, a time of talking over problems concerning the work among the Chinese, and then we prayed. Everyone prayed, and the prayers were long and detailed and no one missed that meeting unless he was ill.

As I look back upon it now, I remember the devotion and sincerity of my own heart, and I still deeply love the friends I made then.

We were all together on our knees in the same room, each with love for the other, and each with a common purpose. But I began to realize we were each making a little speech to the Lord when our turn came. I know we were supposed to pray silently with the one who was praying audibly, but when we all covered the same ground —well, I found that I was trying to think how I could start my prayer with more "colorful" words. How I could put more "action" into my prayer, how I could make it sound more "spiritual," and how I could take hold of the promises with more faith than the others. I wanted to word it differently from the persons who had prayed before me, and make it sound more important and interesting.

God forgive me for the pride that wanted my prayer to

be different! God forgive me for the times I deliberately planned my opening paragraph just to make it sound better than the others!

And God forgive me for the times I used to choose a chair near the bookcases, so that (kneeling in prayer) when things got dull, I could quietly glance through the shelves and make a mental note, and often a penciled note, of the books I wanted to read.

And God forgive me for the times I actually pulled out a book, and using my jacket around my shoulders as a shield, leafed through some of the books during the prayer meeting.

God forgive me, too, for the times I just plain fell asleep on my knees during those long sessions of prayer. After my turn was over, it wasn't too hard to do.

The years of service on the field piled up. The prayer meetings piled up. My rebellions piled up. And yet knowing the sincerity and the depth of the spiritual lives of those with whom I worked and prayed, I couldn't bring myself to admit my rebellion. Neither could I really face the shallowness of my own prayer life.

I was doing the best I knew. Wasn't that all the Lord expected of me?

The third one

Through a near fatal illness and other disrupting events, God began to take care of my rebellions through His great love. He began to teach me to listen to His voice.

This third prayer meeting, which was so simple and yet to be so revolutionary, took place a few months after my time as a mission office secretary ended. I was living in Peiping, China, studying the language and trying to identify myself with the Chinese people in every possible way.

Very soon, a group of high school and college students were asking for instruction in English, and they were interested in reading the English New Testament. Needing help, I called on my long-time friend Mildred Rice, who was living on the same mission compound. We divided the group and met regularly with them.

The young people brought their problems to us, and quite naturally Mildred and I began taking them to the Lord in prayer together.

One never-to-be-forgotten afternoon, we knelt in my little Chinese apartment to pray for several of these students by name, and for the class that evening.

As I remember, Mildred was praying for Ming-lee in a situation that concerned her sister-in-law. Now I'd forgotten to tell Mildred that Ming-lee had sent a little note to me that morning, and that the situation for which Mildred was praying had already been cleared up. Her prayer was already answered and she didn't know it!

Without thinking, I interrupted her prayer, and continued it as mine, "We thank Thee, Lord, that Thou hast already answered that prayer. Ming-lee has already been able to forgive her sister-in-law."

I stopped, startled by my own audacity at interrupting Mildred's prayer. There was a moment of silence, and then with great relief both of us sat back and laughed.

"Why, isn't that something!" said Mildred, meaning both the early answer to her prayer, *and* the natural, spontaneous way in which the news about Ming-lee had popped out.

We settled down to pray again, but with a sense of joy, of lightness, of the Lord's presence very near.

I prayed, "Lord, art Thou trying to teach us something through this incident? Should we give Thee more opportunity while we are praying to get Thy ideas through to us? Would that give the Holy Spirit more opportunity to guide us as we pray?"

Then with the freedom which comes with a new discovery, I stopped praying and spoke to Mildred.

"Do you know what? I believe that Lord taught us something just now! Instead of each of us making a prayer-speech to Him, let's talk things over with Him, back and forth, including Him in it, as we do when we have a conversation."

She took it right up, "Yes, and we could bring up one person or one situation at a time, and both of us pray back and forth about it, until we feel we have touched God, until our hearts are at rest."

I agreed with her thoroughly and said so. But by then I was excitedly remembering something else and had my Bible, hunting a passage in Matthew. There it was.

*Again I say unto you, That if two of you shall agree on
earth as touching any thing that they shall ask, it shall
be done for them of my Father which is in heaven.*

*For where two or three are gathered together in my
name, there am I in the midst of them.*
Matthew 18:19, 20

We were definitely on holy ground and we knew it. In a
few moments of silence then, we both turned our attention
to the Lord Jesus, who being alive and with us and in us
had just told us again,

> *Where two . . . are gathered*
> *in my name*
> *there am I*
> *in the midst of them.*

This time we understood Him in a new way.

Quietly, reverently and with a sharp consciousness that
Another was with us, we began to *converse with Him*
about our friends. All the "padding" of unnecessary
prayer-language slipped away. We spoke face to face,
feeling certain that He cared for the ones we brought to
Him. There seemed to be no need of the final Amen at the
close of each prayer. We were just talking with Him and
with each other. I spoke, and she spoke, and we waited for
Him to reply in that still, small voice within our hearts.

We were in His presence.

We were talking to and with Him.

As we knelt there that afternoon in my Chinese apartment, I experienced a memory flash-back. I remembered
that first "shining moment" when I spoke to Jesus Christ at
the little cottage prayer meeting in North Dakota. After all
these years, He was giving my "shining moment" back to
me, but with a new reality because I was older.

I worshiped Him in silent wonder, knowing that from
now on there need be no more dullness, no more self-conscious conformity, no more imitation.

This was not a new technique we had stumbled upon. It
was too natural and too familiar to be new. Perhaps it was
merely an unexpected turning back to the kind of child-

like communion with Him which God intended in the first place.

We didn't think this far that day. We were just over-joyed.

CHAPTER 2

PRAYER IS A DIALOGUE

The discovery that Mildred Rice and I made that
afternoon in Peiping, China, began to reach deep into our
hearts. It was as though a shade had been raised and a
fresh new day flooded our prayer lives. I don't know why
we didn't go out and tell everyone what had happened.
There was still a holy quietness about having met the Lord
person to person. Perhaps we were afraid that those older
than we might by some chance remark pull the shade
down again.

A great simplification had come, and although we didn't
know it then, we were going to make more and more
discoveries. Discoveries which would heal the rebellious
places in both of us. New insights which would remove
much of the traditionalism which cluttered our prayer
habits. The simplification was: we had become conscious
of His presence with us.

Praying in a conversational tone, one of the first things
we noticed was that unconsciously we were dropping some
of the familiar prayer language. Especially the old Quaker
forms, the beautiful old Quaker forms of thee, thou, and
thy, together with the King James English, with its didst,
dost, wouldst, hadst, walketh, sinneth and so on.

We were speaking to the Lord with the simplicity of a
child talking to its father in his own language. Was it
right? Or was it wrong?

We began to investigate. I was an English major in
college, and remembered that when the King James Bible
was translated, back in the time of Shakespeare, there
were two general kinds of English spoken. A high and low
English. The high English (you, me, yours) was used for
the royal family, nobility and for special ceremonies. The
low English (thou, thee, thy) was used in the home,
intimately with the family, and in addressing God.

As time went on this usage was reversed. The forms
used for royalty became everyday family terms and today

we all say you, me, yours. However, the old terms persisted with the Quakers at all times, and with the religious people at church and at prayer. The King James Bible was translated into English during the Shakespearean period, and so the low form, the familiar endearing family terms were used: thy, thou, thee. And they have come down to us today in our English Bible and in our religious services. The original languages from which our English Bible came to us make no such distinction

I realize that many sincerely feel they are being irreverent in God's presence if they address Him in any form but "Thou." A little of the language background and history will set their minds at rest, and help them relax and be in a more natural attitude for prayer, which is simply conversing with God.

I, for one, love the poetry of the old terms, and always shall. I especially love to hear them used in a Sunday morning worship service. I understand perfectly that you may love them, too, and would rather not make any change. And you can be assured that God understands this also. After all, it isn't the words we say nor how we say them, it is the open heart attitude which God looks for. I don't believe it makes any difference to Him. He simply longs for us to speak person to person with Him without any obstacles between.

If you are beginning to feel that there is a dullness when you pray, or a curtain through which you do not seem able to penetrate, why not deliberately and thoughtfully use everyday English in addressing God? A change, however temporary, usually brings freshness. He is there. He is there with you. He may slip your mind, but you never slip His mind. The different use of a pronoun may be the means through which a new consciousness of His presence will come to you.

Prayer is the expression of the human heart in conversation with God. The more natural the prayer, the more real He becomes. It has all been simplified for me to this extent: prayer is a dialogue between two persons who love each other.

CHAPTER 3

WHAT IS CONVERSATIONAL PRAYER?

The term "conversational prayer" is not an unusual one. Neither is it original. I've found many groups of young people and adults using this direct, honest approach to God. Yet the word conversation needs a fresh defining.

What is conversation?

It is a method which should provide communication between two or more people. Unfortunately, it is usually listed among the lost arts of today.

To understand conversational prayer, it will be a great help if we get the following four points about real conversation clearly in our minds.

1. When we converse, *we become aware*. Aware of the other person, his rights, his privileges, his feeling, and if we converse long enough, his total personality.

2. Good conversation implies that we must take turn about and do it gracefully. When one person does all the talking we call it (if we are polite) a monologue.

3. Finally, it should be clear that to converse *we must all pursue the same subject*, and pursue it by turns. We are, in a sense, the listening and speaking members of a team. We have agreed to agree upon our subject of conversation, and to do this each one must decide what is relevant and important at the moment.

4. To carry on a conversation of any significance or interest, each person must use his memory to recall, his patience to wait, his alertness to jump in, his willingness to get out, and above all his capacity to hold back the disruptive. In other words, *he should be in tune*.

How does all this apply to prayer?

Let me tell you a true story.

Several years ago while I was visiting San Diego State College in California, Ray Williamson, president of the Christian student group, invited me to attend their daily prayer meeting. He pointed to a large tree on the far campus and said, "We meet in a circle around that big tree for fifteen minutes each noon. Meet me here at twelve-thirty sharp and I'll go over with you."

Later, as we walked across the campus toward the big tree, the following conversation took place between Ray and me.

"Is there any special method you follow in your prayer meetings?" I asked.

"Yes, there is," replied Ray. "I usually start, and then the person next to me prays, and we go on around the circle until everyone has prayed."

I reflected on this, knowing that I would very much like to introduce conversational prayer to Ray and his group. But I didn't want to push.

I started with a question. "Ray, how does that give the Holy Spirit opportunity to lead you while you pray?"

He looked at me as we walked. "What do you mean?"

I tried to explain. "Well, you see, it's like this. The Holy Spirit within us moves on our hearts and initiates our concerns and our love, as well as our requests. Could it be possible that in simply going around a circle, humanly speaking, you might 'quench the Spirit'?"

"Quench the Spirit?"

"Yes, by following a set pattern. That makes it difficult for the Spirit to move us as we pray, and to make us aware of what He is saying as we pray. Didn't you ever have a wonderful prayer idea right while the other fellow was praying, and say to yourself, 'Now I must be sure to remember *that* and pray about it when my turn comes,' and then when your turn came you couldn't for the life of you remember what it was?"

Ray laughed. "I'm beginning to see what you're driving at, Ros, and it makes sense. Why don't you tell all of us about it, and show us how? Right now."

"Right now?" I looked to see if he really meant it.

We had already been standing by the big tree for several moments, and the group was gathering.

"Yes, right now," he repeated, and stepping into the circle, called the group together. "Ros has a few keen ideas for us, and I know they will help us have a better prayer meeting."

Briefly I spoke to them, knowing the fifteen minutes would go by quickly.

"Instead of going around tne circle today, let's remember consciously that *the Lord Jesus is right here*, in the center of this circle with us. He promised, 'where two or three are gathered, there am I.' Let's *speak directly to Him*, simply, honestly, just as we talk to anyone in whom we have real confidence. Let's say 'I' when we mean I, and 'we' if we mean the whole group.

"Another important thing is to *pray by subjects*. If someone starts to pray for Joe Blow, two or three of the rest of you feel perfectly free to pray for him, too. Be direct and simple. Then let's wait a moment before introducing a new name. The Spirit will guide us. You can each pray four or five times if you want to, but let's keep to one subject at a time, and pray back and forth. As we open our hearts, the Holy Spirit will guide us concerning who to pray for, what to pray for and when to pray."

Teenagers are quick to grasp new ideas. They were right with me, all of them. I made a quick recap.

"Now remember, the Lord is here. We are speaking to Him. Pray in short sentences, and then let someone else have a chance. He will guide us."

There was silence.

I prayed first. "Lord Jesus, thank You that You are here. You said You would be, and all of us want to thank You, and worship You. (Pause) Guide us now, as to whom we should pray for first."

Ray took it up: "Lord, I want to pray for Tony P., that Italian boy in my swim class. He's my buddy, and I've been wanting to talk with him about You, but I haven't done it yet. Please help me."

A young man across the circle took it next: "Why, Lord, I hadn't any idea Ray was in Tony's swim class. I've already talked to him about You. Bless Ray real good, and give him faith and courage and love for Tony. And help us to work together now."

A girl in the circle gasped audibly. "Oh, how wonderful!" Her spontaneous prayer continued, "Lord, I sit right *next* to *Tony* in an English Lit. Class, and I've already lent him my *HIS* magazine. I was just wishing Tony knew some real Christian guy who'd talk to him. Why, isn't this wonderful! I had no idea that both Ray and Ted knew Tony!"

Several members of the group prayed for these three

and their further contacts with Tony, and for Tony that his heart might be open to receive Christ as his Saviour.

I prayed, "Lord, guide Ray and Ted very definitely. Show them the next step. Show them what you want them to do tomorrow. Help them show Your kind of love to Tony in some definite way."

Ray couldn't wait any longer. He spoke up, and to the whole group. "Say, isn't this great! Hey, this is really neat!" And looking at his wrist watch, "We've got about five minutes more to pray."

Those last five minutes were just as wonderful as the first ten. When the group broke up to go to classes, several of them including Ray walked back with me.

"Ros, tell us more. Why, we were really living just then. This makes prayer alive. What else can you tell us? Is there any more? Shall we just keep on like this?"

"There is just one thing that comes to my mind right now," I replied, not wanting to load them down with too many details which would in any way lessen the joy of their new discovery.

Turning to Ray, I said, "You know what you told me before the meeting about praying around the circle?"

"Yes?"

"Well, when you pray that way you just naturally assume that each person who attends wants to pray, and is willing to pray. Right?"

"Yes," said Ray, slowly thinking it over. "Oh, I think I see what you are driving at, Ros. You mean that there might be someone present who just wants to listen, and *not* pray. Hey, do you suppose anyone who's *not* a Christian might want to come to a prayer meeting?" he finished incredulously.

"That's what I've found," I said, "especially persons with whom I have already talked, and whose hearts are wide open to know the truth. I've known people like that to come, and sometimes the very first time they pray aloud in spite of themselves. The Lord is so near and so real when a group is talking conversationally with Him. And I've seen non-believers walk right into life with Christ just by speaking to Him personally."

Ray was really excited.

"That makes wonderful sense, Ros. After all, when we talk to Christ we're speaking right to truth Himself. He said, 'I am the truth.' If a person really wants to know the truth, what better way is there than to get into a group where it's easier to begin to talk right to God."

That student had struck a deep note.

When we pray, *to whom* are we really speaking?

CHAPTER 4

TO WHOM SHOULD WE PRAY?

To whom should we pray?

Does it make any difference whether we pray to the Father or to the Son, or to the Holy Spirit?

This question is asked over and over. If it does make a difference, we should find out, for God has good reasons for everything that concerns us. If it doesn't make a difference, we should also find out. The fine sensitive relationship which exists between God's Spirit and our spirit needs all the relaxed quietness and receptivity possible. Uninformed ignorance, sluggish unconcern or deadening conformity are all number one enemies which can be sent scampering down their own dark corridors of unbelief.

Is your prayer life alive? Are your prayer times too few and too far between? Have you been bogging down and slowing up? And are you looking back with regret and longing at earlier years when prayer had more meaning to you? I confess this happens periodically with me.

Now and then we should face our need for fresh beginnings. If you have been praying to the Father, and have never addressed the Son in prayer, why not get on speaking terms with Him, too? If you have never addressed the Holy Spirit in prayer, you have a great Counselor who is waiting for you to get acquainted with Him. He knows all about you.

Does it make any difference to whom you pray?

Whose presence are you aware of when you pray? Is your heart at all affected by the name or names by which you address God when you pray? Or are you more concerned about the content of your prayer? Or perhaps your concern may be just to get it over with, so you can relax again.

I want to tell you about a college girl who had been completely unaware of the name she was using when she prayed, and of the amazing difference it made in her relationship to God when she did become aware.

Marion was a college sophomore when I first met her, and was one of a small group of girls who met to plan and pray with me about how best to present Jesus Christ to their friends on campus. Each noon we met for a short time of prayer. We were learning to pray conversationally. After I'd heard her pray once, I was concerned. After the second time I'd heard her, I prayed, "Lord, if you want me to speak with Marion and give her a few pointers, put it into her heart to come and see me." (I believe in definite, time-limit, faith-sized requests for some things, and will develop this subject in a later chapter.)

That very night there was a knock at my door. It was Marion. I was glad to see her and told her so. I even told her that I'd asked the Lord to send her.

"You did?" she asked. "Why?"

"Because I see a great God-potential in you and I think a little talk might help bring it out. You won't mind, will you, Marion, if I talk with you about something I've noticed?"

She told me to go right ahead.

"Marion, to whom do you pray?"

She hesitated a moment, "I guess I pray to the Lord Jesus."

"Do you?" I waited a moment to let her think. "What do you call Him?"

"Uh—uh—Dear Lord Jesus," she said uncertainly.

"Well, tell me, Marion, do you do this both in your own private prayers and when you pray with others?"

"Why, uh—yes, I think I do," Marion looked a little puzzled. "Ros, why are you asking me this? Go ahead and tell me."

So I told her. I had taken the liberty of timing her prayer the second time I'd heard her. And I had a reason. The prayer lasted one minute, and in that time she had used the name "God" thirty-three times! She has used His Name as a punctuation mark, and not as though she were speaking to a real, living Person.

I gave her an example of the way she prayed, so she would understand: "O God, we thank You, God, that we can come into Your Presence, God. God, we need You today, God. God, will You help us, O God, to live for You today, God."

She was embarrassed and surprised, but fortunately very open. We had a comfortable talk on the subject, and then she asked, "Could we pray again now?" We did, and this time, by her own choice, she started, "Dear Lord Jesus ..." instead of her habitual, "Dear God ..." She prayed slowly, thoughtfully, with many pauses, and used His Name meaningfully. She *was* speaking to Someone, *He* was there!

Suddenly she looked up, with tears, "Oh, Ros, I feel as if I've become a Christian all over again! I didn't know what I was doing before. I guess I was praying to be praying, if there is such a thing. I didn't really know to whom I was praying. Now I know. It's Jesus Christ!"

In my own efforts to learn the true meaning of prayer, and to recognize His presence, I personally have found it more helpful to address most of my prayers to the Lord Jesus. And yet there are times when I find myself praying to the Father, or to the Holy Spirit. I searched the New Testament with this one thought in mind: to find when and why each member of the Trinity was addressed. I had a page in my notebook for each, and from this study I gained confidence and knowledge.

I am not trying to give you a pat theological answer. I am only trying to give you the simple answers I found for myself in regard to whom I may address my prayer. But out of this study I have also found a simplicity concerning the whole Christian faith. I discovered that when this mystifying subject of the Trinity is brought up and talked about and explained (inasmuch as we are able), it begins of its own accord to form the basis of our belief in the Person of Jesus Christ.

There is one God. Not three. He is three Persons but one in essence and substance. The dictionary definition of essence is this: That *in being* which underlies all outward manifestations and is permanent and unchangeable. In other words, the very substance of.

Why has God shown Himself to us in three Persons? Where did this idea originally come from?

Jesus Christ Himself taught us (mainly in the Gospel of John) that He and the Father are one. *Jesus Christ is the Father defined.* No one called God "Father" before Jesus came. The complete fifth chapter of John is a discourse on the equality of the Father and the Son. No one knew what God was really like until in the Person of Jesus of Nazareth, He came to visit this earth and show Himself as He really is.

Where does the Holy Spirit come into the picture? Jesus said (and I paraphrase from John 14:16-20): I am going away to my Father, but I will send the Comforter, the Spirit of truth to be with you forever. I will not leave you helpless orphans, I will come to you. In that day you will know that I am in my Father, and you in me, and I in you.

Paul tells us in II Corinthians 3:17 that the Holy Spirit is the Spirit of the Lord Jesus in us.

If you seem to be having trouble with understanding that three persons can be of one essence, here is an illustration which has helped me. The compound H_2O is found in three forms, gas, liquid and solid (air, water, ice) but they are all composed of the same basic elements—two atoms of hydrogen and one of oxygen. Each has a significance and use of its own, but all are composed of exactly the same elements. There is no contradiction among them, just as there is no contradiction among the members of the Godhead.

From an old Scotch Presbyterian book I copied a diagram of the Trinity which I have found most helpful. See page 89. Notice that the name GOD is all inclusive and when you start from the center of the circle, the fact that they are all one becomes evident: God is the Father, God is the Son, God is the Spirit. But go around the outer edge of the circle, and you find the Father is not the Son, the Son is not the Spirit, the Spirit is not the Father. Their one essence is shown at the center, and their three personalities are shown at the circumference.

Why has God shown Himself to us in three Persons?

God is the great Eternal Being, and we are so limited in all our spiritual concepts that He has given us three different glimpses of Himself, through three different Personalities, but the three are One.

I believe that God must have anticipated this human confusion of ours about Himself. This is surely one of the reasons He visited this earth in the Person of Jesus Christ. As we study Christ's life, death and resurrection, we find ourselves being overcome by the certain knowledge of God's true character.

It is important for us to be able to think of our God as a Person, not an idea, or a principle or even a spiritual concept. It must follow that whatever name we use for Him, that name must have some real meaning for us. There are literally hundreds of names for God in both the Old and New Testament.

How many names do you have for the person most beloved on earth to you? Does one mean any more than another? The reason is usually a significant one.

We neither offend Him nor pacify Him by the name we choose to use when we speak to Him. His love is unchanging. It is not at all dependent on us or the phrases we happen to use.

I know Jesus taught us to "Pray to your Father who is in secret." When He was on earth, He prayed to His Father. He taught us to say, "Our Father, which art in heaven." Most of the time He was concealing His own personal glory and identity, both of which have now been revealed. During His earthly days He voluntarily became dependent upon His Father, though from eternity they have been equal.

Jesus invited us to pray in His Name. He assured us that He alone has power to give us eternal life. He taught that all the Father is and has are His. "The Father judgeth no man, but hath committed all judgment unto the Son: That all men should honour the Son, even as they honour the Father. He that honoureth not the Son honoureth not the Father which hath sent him" (John 5:22, 23).

Jesus Christ was worshiped by those who knew who He was, both during His earthly life and after His resurrection. One of the central themes of the Book of Revelation is that the Lamb will be the object of our worship through all eternity.

For an Old Testament look at the names of the coming God-Man, there is Isaiah 9:6: "For unto us a child is born, unto us a son is given: and the government shall be upon His shoulder: and his name shall be called Wonderful, Counsellor, The mighty God, The everlasting Father, The Prince of Peace."

Paul tells us that every knee in heaven and on earth and under the earth will bow at the Name of Jesus.

Is Jesus Christ God? Your answer to this question will determine your attitude toward Him. Is the deity of the Son of God actual? Is it Scriptural? A positive answer to these questions has meant the beginning of a personal relationship with Jesus Christ to many inquiring hearts.

Before I came to know Stella Newbill of Seattle (she is now my good friend) she had been seeking God for some time. It was easy to come to the point. "Stella, I hear you have been reading Unity. Are you receiving any help?"

"Who told you, Ros? I'd be interested to know," said Stella.

So I told her and she smiled. "Yes, I have been reading Unity, because I need to have some prayers answered. But I still have one big question. Is Jesus Christ God?"

From there we began a conversation neither of us will ever forget. An hour or so later, as we knelt together in prayer, Stella quietly in her own words, and for the first time in her life, acknowledged Jesus Christ as her Lord and her God. A personal relationship began for her that day because, knowing who God really is, she could put her trust in Him.

For the past two years she has been an amazingly creative and fruitful witness to Jesus Christ in her community. One of the first persons to be reached for Christ through Stella was her husband, Art. Now both of them are strong and peaceful in the midst of a physical illness which I have seen defeat persons who have been Christians for most of their lives. They are both sure of God's ultimate intentions toward them because they know what Jesus Christ is like, and they know that He and the Father are one.

Our God is infinite, but we are so earthbound that He has done everything possible to help us grasp and understand something of His eternal dimensions. He has given us three views of Himself, and yet there is more. Like the vast ocean stretching away, there is so much more.

I am forever convinced that anyone who comes to the place of realizing that God and Jesus Christ are one and the same, has reached the potential of a new plateau in prayer. Somehow it is easy to speak to Jesus Christ. After all, we know that He knows what it feels like to be us.

Wherefore in all things it behoved him to be made like unto his brethren... (Hebrews 2:17).

CHAPTER 5

PRAYER BEGINS A NEW RELATIONSHIP

In this chapter I would like to tell you how conversational prayer, or conversing with God, has provided the simple way by which people have come into the Kingdom of God. The simplicity of responding person to person to Jesus Christ seems to break down all barriers. Yet it is not prayer that is emphasized, nor is prayer the important thing. Christ is the center, and prayer is the means by which we begin to respond to Him. In a moment I'll share with you two stories which illustrate what I mean.

But first let us think back about the things we have already learned about conversing with God.

We know to whom we are speaking. We are not talking with an unknown God, but to the God-Man, Jesus Christ, who was in all points tempted like as we are, so that we can feel freer to come to Him with our temptations. We have come to a clearer knowledge of the greatness of our God, who has shown Himself to us as the great Three in One.

We have also discussed some of the things that keep us from intimate conversation with Him: The lack of knowledge of who Jesus Christ is, failure to remember He is constantly present with us; the language barriers, the tradition-bound prayer habits, self-consciousness or desire for the approval of others.

In order to overcome these barriers we need not only to read, but also to begin to put what we have read into daily prayer practice. We need to learn the art of conversation. We need to learn to pray in His Presence, and to let Him speak with us, to be in tune with Him until we are willing to hear what He has to say to us.

There is an intimate relationship between the Shepherd and the sheep which is always initiated by the Shepherd Himself. But there is something for the sheep to do when he enters the fold. He has to be willing to hear and respond to the Shepherd's voice. Frequently we need the help of one or two other "sheep" who already know His voice in order to make our response a complete one. *We need to learn to pray with one another.* We are all sheep of His pasture, and we need to be together.

But more is involved than merely being willing to pray together. How does one *know* when he is in the fold? *When* does one receive eternal life? The answer is simple. When he comes to Jesus. When he feels that *need* which the Spirit has put into his heart, and when he begins to respond to Jesus Christ, as the God who can forgive his sins and make him a member of His fold.

This brings us to those wonderful words which the Lord gave us in John 10:27. When *do* we become His sheep?

I remember Grace, a brilliant Chinese university student, who was about to complete her study for her doctorate in chemistry. Her chief concern for weeks had been the fact that she wanted to be a Christian and was not. One day we sat together at a study table talking about what Jesus Christ had already done on the Cross, and I promised her that because He is alive, speaking directly to Him would bring her the assurance she needed. Still she hesitated.

We turned to John's Gospel and read chapter 10 verse 27 together: "My sheep hear my voice and I know them, and they follow me; And I give them eternal life. . . ." I asked her to notice the sequence of the verbs. My sheep *hear* my voice. They *follow* me. I *give* them eternal life. Then I asked, when did they become His sheep, before or after Jesus gave them eternal life? We looked again. The first step is to hear His voice and begin to follow the Shepherd, and then He does all the giving.

She admitted she had heard His voice. But when did this "sheep" belong to Jesus? There it was, right in the beginning of the verse, *My* sheep. Because He already considered her His, she was able to hear His voice! Suddenly she saw it from His viewpoint. This is a mystery I cannot explain, but in His great eternal knowledge, He knows when to call us. There is no past, present or future with the Lord. It is all an eternal *now* with Him.

There was silence at the table where we sat. We bowed our heads, and I said, "Thank You Lord, for showing Grace Your viewpoint." And she prayed, "Lord Jesus, I want to thank You. This is my first time to speak to You.

So You've been here all along!" Then I thanked Him again. And quite naturally, Grace prayed again and thanked Him for forgiving her sins and for giving her eternal life.

For a moment neither of us spoke. Then she began to pray for her family and for her friends. The barrier was down. Speaking directly to Him had made Him a real Person to her. Knowing, finally, that Jesus Christ had loved her from the beginning, there was only one thing left to do, and that was respond by speaking to Him.

Last Year in New York City I was having lunch in the Manhattan Hotel Coffee Shop with a professional woman who had come to know her need of Jesus Christ through adverse circumstances. She tells the story in her own words in the copy she sent me of a letter she wrote to her mother:

"Christ was always a waiting figure to me, who charmed and glowed, but still it seemed He always was 'outside me,' always slipping away from me. It seemed to me He was a waiting potential, nothing more: And I was sure it was His fault. Ros said, 'But Marj, have you *asked* Him to come in, have you said, "Welcome, abide with me" to Him even once?' No, I just hadn't, Mother. Never, not once: He scared me rather. For no reason at all. Ros said, 'Do you want to, now?' I said yes, and so help me, with her eyes open, so it looked for all the world like we were having a casual coffee shop conversation, Ros prayed. And then I said, 'Lord Jesus, I love You, too.' And meant it fully, with all my heart. That is why the past two months or so have been so different as to be beyond belief. Now there is a sheer, keen joy of living which I never really had before. I don't know much yet, and may make mistakes, but I know Jesus Christ will fix those up, too."

I have included the experiences of these two women in this chapter since I have observed that a pious prayer in an emotionally charged atmosphere can turn some people the other direction, while an open, natural conversation with the Lord Himself, who is always right there with us, can make a hard step easier. It is not easy to turn the controls of your life over to Another when you can't see Him. But when you can know He's there and speak with Him and to Him naturally, the barriers go down.

The response of your heart to His initial love for you releases your love for Him.

You discover that He has long sought you, called to you, prepared for you, loved you. And now you know the way into the fold: Response to the Shepherd Himself, Jesus Christ.

Have you responded to Him?

Have you spoken to Him, simply, naturally, out of the need of your heart? In your own words?

He is there.

If you are interested in Him, you can come. Your very interest proves that you have heard His voice. And He has said:

Everyone who has heard ... comes to me.

Further Bible reading on the subject of this chapter: Matthew 11:25-30; John 6:35-51; John 10.

CHAPTER 6

WHY PRAY ALOUD TOGETHER?

Why should I pray aloud with someone else? Doesn't Jesus Himself say "Enter into thy closet, and pray to thy Father which is in secret?"

Yes, Jesus did say this. And "Why should I pray aloud with someone else?" could very well be the question you are asking. I am aware that so far we have seemed to emphasize group prayer, but all that has been said may apply to our personal devotions as well. There are many reasons for this emphasis on praying together which I shall continue to share; but I do understand your question about the necessity of praying with others.

Jesus taught us to go into our closets and pray to our Father in secret. Have you read the verses that go with this one? You will find them in Matthew 6:1-14. Jesus is warning us against praying for the approval of others, and telling us that there is only One to whom we should pray.

Since you object to praying with others because of Jesus' words, "Enter into your closet" do you then deeply desire to keep His words? And do you often enter into your closet and pray in secret? And do you find new life and new love through meeting Him there?

I know these are pointed questions, but unless we are honest with ourselves here, we can go on and on, missing the wonder the Lord Jesus has for us.

Almost every real revelation about Himself and His will has come to me *after* He has broken down some barrier which has been erected. Erected in simple self-defense or fear. Erected because of environment or background. It is quite possible that these barriers are among the "mountains" about which the Lord Jesus speaks in Mark 11:23. "Whoever says to this mountain, 'Be taken up and thrown into the sea!' and entertains no inner doubt, but believes that what he says will happen, it shall be so for him" (Berkeley).

We shall talk more about removing "mountains" in the

chapter on faith-sized requests. However, we can look at some of them right here, honestly and openly, and we can begin to see them disintegrate and slip away into the "sea." The mountain of fear exists mainly behind closed doors of aloneness. Open the door, share with others, and the chances are you will look in vain for your "mountain."

Jesus did teach us to go into our closets and pray to our Father in secret, because He knows that when we shut out everyone else and concentrate on being with Him, on being conscious of Him, our heart-wounds are healed and we are made whole. There, alone in the quietness, He can speak to us and comfort us and guide us and pour His fresh life and love into us. Praying is like eating; you must eat for yourself, no one else can do it for you.

But Jesus Christ also taught us to pray together and to say, "Our Father which art in heaven." This is the only entire prayer He gave us. Yet He made many references to prayer.

He said: "Keep on asking and it will be given you." "Whatever you ask for in prayer, believe—trust and be confident—that it is granted to you, and you will [get it]." "—I Myself will grant—whatever you may ask in My name." "Ask and keep on asking and you will receive, so that your joy (gladness, delight) may be full and complete" (Matthew 7:7; Mark 11:24; John 14:13; 16:24, Amplified).

More than any other teaching Jesus gave us on prayer, I think I love the one Matthew recorded in chapter 18, verses 19 and 20, and the surrounding verses. Before writing this chapter I read them again from seven different versions and translations: King James, Revised Standard, Amplified New Testament, Berkeley, Lamsa, Phillips and Williams. They all throw new light on Matthew 18:19, 20 but I want to quote from the direct, simple Williams' translation: "Again, I tell you, if only two of you on earth agree on what they pray for, they will get it from my Father in heaven. For wherever two or three have met as my disciples, I am right there with them."

Why pray together? Because Jesus promised that when two of His disciples (that means us today) meet to pray, He will be there with them. Our risen, living Lord said and meant what He said: "I am there, right among them" (Phillips). "There am I in the midst of them" (King James).

In a particular way, in a particular promise, *He is present.*
I have experienced it again and again, and so can you.

Why pray together?

Because Jesus knows that the problems of life press in
upon us when we are alone until the spirit is almost
broken; the mind refuses to accept reality and so escapes
into a world of its own. Burdens shared become lighter.
"Bear one another's burdens," said Paul. Before I learned
the secret of prayer together, I thought that my burdens
were greater than anyone else's burdens. Now I know they
aren't and now I know a way to help instead of always
wanting to be helped.

Why pray together?

Because as we pray the Spirit of our Lord has our
attention. He is always conscious of us, but we need to
focus our attention and our consciousness upon Him. Then
He can whisper to us the love plans He has for us.
Sometimes these directions come to two or more persons in
the group at the same time. We find ourselves in total
agreement in all that we are asking. This leaves no room
for wavering, for double-mindedness or for doubt. We
have agreed in His presence, and He Himself has given us
that agreement.

Why pray together?

Because His great heart of love longs and yearns to give
us all that we need, whether that need is spiritual, mental,
emotional, physical or material. I believe He gives us all
He can give, without our direct asking; but when we are
consciously in His presence He softens our hearts and our
minds, and we find ourselves being changed and enabled
to receive. When we pray together we become bold and
honest, and ask for things we never intended asking for at
all.

Why pray together?

Praying with other people gives us new sisters and new
brothers in Christ. The more we pray with other people
the more we begin to trust them, and the more honest we
all can be about our personal needs. Self-consciousness
drops away and we can pray about our real problems, not
just surface ones. Genuine "togetherness" is a God-given
state, and hearts are joined in His presence. We can
depend upon that presence because He has said, "I am
right there with them."

If all this and more is waiting for us when we pray with one another and with Him, why is it that so few persons today meet to pray together? We spend hours in time-consuming pleasant conversation. We talk for an hour on the telephone. We all know how to talk. And we talk. Why then do we find so many excuses not to talk with the Lord Jesus, and with each other in His presence?

Even though we practice it little, we believe in prayer and we want to know more about prayer. We want to know more about the simplicity of praying. In a survey conducted on "Sermons America Wants to Hear" by *This Week* magazine, the number one choice was: "How Can I Make Prayer More Effective?" The results of this poll are no surprise to me. Everywhere I go I find a growing interest in prayer.

At this writing, I have just returned from a Michigan church where we held pre-Easter meetings. My associate, Eugenia Price, brought the evening message. The pastor wanted an invitation following the message, but was afraid the people wouldn't go along with it.

This plan came to our minds while Genie and I were actually praying together: She would announce an "after-service" in which I would give simple instruction on prayer, using material from this book. We felt that only those with real needs would come. The first night I set out ten chairs in the room adjoining the church sanctuary. To our amazement, seventy persons crowded into that room! It was the same night after night. Many of them had never prayed aloud and did not particularly want to pray aloud in front of anyone else. But most of the people did pray—simply, honestly and directly from their hearts.

During the week we were there, families which had never prayed together before began to speak to God conversationally in their homes. A regular church prayer meeting has begun again at the request of the people and the minister. Comfort and togetherness were given to lonely hearts. We left with the certainty that things have only just begun to happen in that Michigan church.

I was more convinced than ever that people do want to pray, and all that is needed is simple instruction at the personal level, and an opportunity to pray. We don't learn how to pray in six easy lessons, we learn to pray by praying.

But, you say, I am not in that Michigan community, and there is no group of people in my church or town with whom I can pray. Then begin to "ask" for someone with whom you can pray. Ask and believe that God can and will give you at least one person with whom you may pray aloud.

Maybe you still have an unconscious block about praying aloud, which will not yield. In the first five chapters of this book we have already talked about many of the problems concerning praying aloud. Perhaps it will help you to look at them again. One of them is bound to be yours:

Chapter 1. Self-defense, what others think, wanting the approval of others, wanting to be "spiritual," fear of imperfection in praying, fear of weeping.

Chapter 2. Long wearisome prayers, stilted in language and static in content, uncreative and without life.

Chapter 3. The language barrier, the King James tongue twisters, the far-awayness of God because you may think He cannot appreciate English as it is spoken today.

Chapter 4. The haziness of your concept of the Triune God. It is difficult to pray to a God you do not know. Prayer to the Father may seem stiff and formal because you fail to understand the identity of the Son and of the Holy Spirit.

Chapter 5. The impossibility of speaking intimately (as in prayer) to One with whom we have no relationship. Perhaps your need is to invite Him into your heart, to make a definite commitment of yourself to Him, to believe in Him personally, and to believe that He is a Person whom you can trust.

All the above problems are answered in each of the chapters mentioned. At least they are answered in a way that helped me, and opened the way for me to approach God through Jesus Christ.

The real basis for not wanting to pray with someone else (aside from not wanting to answer the call of the Good Shepherd and come under His authority and His care) is usually human pride. Pride is the basis of all self-consciousness, which in turn is one of the products of being a so-called adult. Children pray easily without self-conflict or self-consciousness. Jesus taught us that we must become like little children to enter, and to live within, the Kingdom of Heaven. As adults we become aware of ourselves and our real or imagined abilities, and will go to any lengths to erect defenses to keep from exposing ourselves as we are.

Do you really want to learn to pray with others? Do you recognize what it is that is holding you back? Then you are "on the way" and it is the Good Shepherd Himself who is leading you.

Anyone who belongs to Jesus Christ, confessing Him as Lord and Saviour, can be delivered from fear of praying in public. The first step is to ask Him to deliver you from this fear. Read II Timothy 1:7. "For God hath not given us the spirit of fear; but of power, and of love, and of a sound mind." Let us ask and receive the gifts He has for us, and refuse all else, in the power of His name.

Dietrich Bonhoeffer, in his book, *Life Together* (Harpers) helped me tremendously. I defeat my purpose for instance, if I pat myself on the back after I pray aloud, and say to myself, "My, you certainly prayed a good prayer that time!"

A prayer life full of self-conceit and pride would rise no higher than the top of my head, and certainly there would be no unconscious outreach in love to my brother or sister in that prayer group. I would be thinking only of making a good impression, and the unconscious result of such an attitude both upon myself and upon others would leave little room for love.

Go ahead and stumble in your prayers, go ahead and cry. Out of your very weakness your brother is made strong. Out of your own weakness you are made strong by Christ. Out of the inadequacy of your prayer, the inability to express yourself, the shame of your tears, and the urgency of your need, you meet the Saviour who understands you. You are comforted and your brother is strengthened. Out of this weakness your brother, hearing and observing that you are in no better state than he, becomes strong. He is encouraged by your so-called failures that he, too, may meet the Lord in his weakness.

If I pray a "spiritual" sounding, well-padded prayer of which I am proud, who is helped by it? Neither I nor my brother.

Whenever two or three are gathered together, said Jesus, *I am right there with them.*

Wherever two or three are gathered with the Lord, there He is, with all His love revealed and exposed. How? In and by and through one another. And where there is love there is healing. Wherever Jesus Christ is present eternal love is present. When my attention is turned toward Him, and my prayer directed to Him, then His love heals my heart, and I am ready to pray, in love, for my brother or my sister.

For wherever two or three have met as my disciples,
I am right there with them (Williams).

CHAPTER 7

WHY PRAY ALONE?

In the last chapter we thought together about some of the results which come when we pray together. In this chapter we want to think about the important place which secret prayer should have in every believer's life.

There are many important things which the Lord wants to give us which (psychologically) result only from group prayer. To refresh our minds, here are a few of the things we found as we looked into the meaning of Matthew 18: 19, 20.

When we meet to pray with someone else, *the Lord is present* as a third party. Together we learn to talk, to Him and with Him, in openness and simplicity and without self-consciousness. We leave our heavy burdens at His feet by sharing and agreeing together. Our fears and anxious worries melt away. He speaks and together we learn to listen. He gives us guidance and direction and spiritual healing. He makes us ready to receive all He has to give to us. We acquire new brothers and sisters. We belong to a new family and we begin to learn to take spiritual family responsibilities for one another.

One of the most important things we learned was that even our weaknesses become sources of strength when we are consciously there in His presence, because *need* is the golden door of opportunity through which our Saviour meets us face to face.

All this and more comes from just being there together. All this and more comes from being there, consciously in His presence. All this and more awaits those who will answer His call to come apart with Him—alone.

"Rise up, my love, my fair one, and come away. For lo, the winter is past . . . The flowers appear on the earth; the time of the singing of birds is come, and the voice of the turtle is heard in our land. . . . Arise, my love, my fair one, and come away. O my dove, that art in the clefts of the rock, in the secret places of the stairs, let me see thy countenance, let me hear thy voice" (Song of Solomon 2:10-14).

The Good Shepherd knows what His sheep need. They need the pastures of being together with one another, but they also need the quiet waters of intimate security—security which comes from being alone with Him in the secret places.

"My sheep hear my voice, and they follow me."

When have you heard His voice and followed Him into His secret place? When have you found rest in just being with Him?

Being human, we tend to be heavy-handed in one direction or the other. Depending upon our personality bents, some of us tend either toward always being with people or always being alone. These preferences carry over directly into our prayer life. It is just as eccentric to leave all praying until prayer meeting night as it is to insist that religion is a private matter and do all our praying alone. Actually it is quite possible to become so ingrown in our relationships with God that we "escape" to the closet, labeling it virtue.

Recently such a young woman came for counseling, and I discovered that due to strained and broken relationships with loved ones, she had almost entirely withdrawn from people. She was finding her "comfort" alone in her room, meditating and reading and praying. But the results of all this were introspective and unhealthy.

None of us should hide behind the alibi that "this is the way I am." None of us should say that due to our own personality, we are unable to be at ease in the presence of other believers, or that we are unable to pray with them. By the same token none of us should say that we cannot learn to be alone in a room for an hour or more with God. In time and with willingness anyone can learn to do both. To have one without the other is like having day without night. They complement one another, they help us to become whole persons.

But the Shepherd will not drive you. He will not drive you either to share the joys of praying with others, nor will He drive you to the intimacy of prayer alone. He will wait. He will draw you and keep drawing you until you begin to respond. He waits for you to begin to speak to Him, and to respond from love's freedom, not from love's compulsion.

When you are ready, you will find that He has been waiting for you, conscious of you all the time.

There are several practical points which may help you to make this practice of secret prayer part of your daily life.

1. Have a definite place to pray alone. Every time you pass that place, whether it is by a chair, or your bedside, an unused room, a little closet, your desk or your car, you will be reminded that both physical and spiritual refreshment await you there.

2. Anticipate meeting One who loves you in a personal intimate way. Before you arrive at this special place, let your mind constantly say, "I am going to meet Him, I am going to be consciously aware of Him." After you are there, say: "Here in this quiet place, He can show me Himself. I am His. I can put aside all else and worship You, my Lord, and my God."

3. Let your prayers be semi-audible. You *are* speaking to a Person, and hearing your own voice will keep your thoughts centered on Him, although sometimes there will be only deep unspoken torrents of love and adoration welling up from within.

4. Use a daily devotional book, and use some kind of study book to give you needed direction in your daily Bible reading. (See footnote below.)

Here it might be well to ask yourself, What does worship really mean to me? I fail to understand how it is possible to give the Lord full attention when we are alone, unless we know something of the real meaning of conscious worship.

In my not-too-long-ago-do-it-yourself approach to God, I used to congratulate myself on the fact of my daily faithfulness in having a Quiet Time. My spiritual temperature went up or down as I did or did not keep my Quiet Time. And when I spoke to others, I gave the impression that I always had a successful Quiet Time, and was, of course, always "victorious." This was far from the truth.

The truth, I am now joyfully discovering, is that even

Daily devotional books: *My Utmost for His Highest*, Oswald Chambers (Dodd-Mead); *Our Daily Walk*, F. B. Meyer (Zondervan); *Share My Pleasant Stones*, Eugenia Price (Zondervan).

Guides to Bible Reading: Scripture Union (3 Cawthra Street, Toronto, Ont., Canada). *Who Is This Man?*, Rosalind Rinker (Zondervan).

when I am false, He is true. I change, but He never
changes. Have you discovered that no matter what you are
like, He is always the same? His faithfulness is as sure as
the law of gravitation. This discovery will turn your
attention away from yourself to Him. And then, when you
stop paying attention to yourself, you find that He is your
victory. He is the Giver, and with Him come all the gifts
that you have been seeking piecemeal! They are all in
Him.

Through all the years of my do-it-yourself period, with
all my many attempts to "die to sin" I was still alive, and
very much alive. Through all my sincere attempts to
"abide in Christ" I was still too often expressing my own
selfish spirit, and not His spirit of holy love.

And then I discovered—worship.

True worship takes place within the quietness of the
individual. True worship is subjection to Jesus Christ. True
worship depends upon the kind of God you worship. True
worship is not conditioned by any religious atmosphere. It
is like a well of water springing up from within the heart
of the lover for the Beloved.

It took a negative form of worship to open my eyes to
the meaning of true worship. I was visiting my first
Chinese temple in the city of Shanghai. Inside, it was dark
and shadowy and lined with double rows of dusty idols on
heavy pedestals. At the far end was a tall loft and a giant
gilded idol was set among heavy draperies that covered all
but its feet. A Chinese woman came in to worship. She
burned incense, she waved it before the dumb idol, she
prostrated her little self before the huge fifty-foot god and
waited for an answer. Was there any? There was none.

So that was "worshiping idols." Suddenly I knew that
the God I worshiped was alive, that He was a Person who
responded to me and to whom I could respond.

But did I worship the Ever-Living One?

Did I really know what worship meant?

Suddenly I wanted to get out of that temple and go
home. I wanted to go into my own room and close
the door and lock it. I wanted to get on my knees with my
face to the floor, like that little Chinese woman. But unlike
her, I wanted to worship the living God who created and
sustains all life, and who has revealed Himself as He is in

the Person of Jesus Christ. I wanted to be quiet and let all
the love and adoration and worship of my heart go out to
Him in a way that I had never done before.

Worship to me had meant "Sunday morning worship
service." I wonder sometimes now what that means, for I
have learned that it is in silence, holy silence, that my
heart pours out its best love and worship to my Lord and
my God. I have learned that worship is that honor, respect
and adoration a small earthling like me can feel and give
to the Almighty Creator.

My concept of worship has grown and deepened, and
this is now the most important part of my Quiet Time. It is
out of this personal worship that I find myself ready to
share and be a part of a group of God's children.

In the Appendix of this book, you will find a seven-day
study entitled, "Aids to Personal Worship." This material
was prepared in booklet form for use with college students
on the west coast, and is a simple, step by step devotional
guide to personal worship. It is a study of God's character.
Each day you will make use of what you learned the day
before, and you will learn to worship.

It is when I am worshiping God that my heart is
cleansed, that I am assured of His great love which has
taken full responsibility for me. It is then that the Cross
and the sufferings of Christ arouse my heart to know more
and more of the depth of His love. It is when I am
worshiping and lost in wonder, and my conscious and
unconscious self pours out love, that I become a whole
person. It is when I have thus worshiped God that I begin
to know the meaning of "Abide in me and I in you."

Before I grasped this there was endless self-effort, now
it is a matter of resting in Christ.

CHAPTER 8

WHAT IS FAITH?

"I don't seem to be able to get answers to my prayers the way other people do. I wish I had that kind of faith!"

Have you ever said that? Until we begin to understand the laws under which faith operates, we cannot expect to make much progress. Understanding is knowledge, and knowledge is power.

Is faith a special gift which is given to some and not to others? What is the source of faith? Is it for all of us? Are God's answers given to those who possess faith, and withheld from those who do not have it? Can one know whether he has faith or not? Is receiving conditioned only by how much faith we have, or are there other important factors? Isn't it true that sin in our lives hinders God from answering prayer? And don't we have to exercise our faith so it will become stronger?

The answers to all these questions are found in the prayer promises which abound in the New Testament. They are also found in the gospel accounts of desperate men and women who made their way into the presence of Jesus Christ.

Mark records a miracle for us in the fifth chapter of his gospel which has helped me a great deal in understanding more about what faith is and how it operates. In this story there are five lessons which begin to unfold the mysteries of faith, the faith which asks and receives.

The first one is God's willingness to give us what we ask for. The second one is what to ask for. The third one is how to ask. The fourth is the important place "desire" plays in asking. The fifth is the necessity for a "point of contact."

1. God's Willingness

If you are not familiar with the story of the woman who touched the hem of His garment, turn to Mark 5:21-43 and read the whole story. Her healing caused an interruption in Jesus' journey to the home of an influential man with a critically ill daughter. And because of that interruption, the daughter was dead when they arrived. Jesus knew this beforehand, but still the true character of God was displayed in His love and kindness to the woman as well as to the distraught father.

Jesus Christ and the Father are One. Jesus is the Word, and "the Word became Human and lived a little while among us, and we actually saw His glory . . ." (John 1:14, Williams.) God Himself is willing to be interrupted when He is on the way to meet the desperate need of Jairus, because He knows He not only can heal this sick daughter, He can raise her from the dead.

God is willing to give us what we ask for, even if it means a delay in His day's journey, and even if it means death at the end of the journey. He is willing to do this because of what He is like. He can handle one as well as the other. His eternal love and kindness and tender mercy go far beyond the care of an earthly father and mother. He is more willing to give than we are to receive. No eye has seen nor has any ear heard all the things that God has prepared for those who love Him. It was John Newton who wrote:

> Come, my soul, thy suit prepare:
> Jesus loves to answer prayer;
> He, Himself has bid thee pray,
> Therefore will not say thee nay.

Did you ever make a study of the prayer promises in the New Testament with the idea of finding out what God is like? I could copy these promises and fill several pages, but doing it yourself always brings surprises. Writing them down and looking at them helps you find words or ideas which are alike in all these passages. Here are some references,* but no doubt you could find many more in your own Bible concordance.

After such a study, one word seemed to light up for me.

---

* Prayer References: Matthew 6:8; 7:7-12; 18:18-20; 21:21, 22; Mark 11:22-26; Luke 11:9-11; John 14:12-14; 15:7; 16-24; James 1:5-8; I John 3:20-22, 5:14, 15.

See if you can find it here for yourself, in this next paragraph which blends several promises.

All are freely invited to ask and to receive. We are told that we will receive what we ask for if we search and knock and ask. We are told to ask in Christ's name and He will do whatever we ask. We are told to abide or to find our reason for living, in Christ, and then we can have whatever we ask for. We are also told not to doubt, and to believe that we are going to get what we have asked for.

In all of these promises the word that gets our attention is the little word "ask." Think what that means! God has told us *to ask* so that He may relieve the intolerable burdens of fear, tragedy and loneliness. The burdens of illness, poverty and injustice. God has told us to ask so that He may pour His gifts into our hearts and lives without measure.

If there is anyone reading who is not convinced that God is willing to give good gifts to those who call on Him, let that person finish this chapter before giving up.

Jesus was on the way to the dying daughter of a famous man when an unknown woman touched His clothing. He not only cured her, but He tenderly said, "Daughter . . . go in peace, be free from your disease."

There is no unwillingness in God—He will give us anything that we ask. His eternal character is always on the side of love. It is only when our asking is out of line with holy love that He withholds our answer. Withholding can be holy love, also.

2. *What Shall We Ask For?*

That brings us to our second point. What shall we ask for? And is there any special way of asking which will bring a sure answer?

Back to the sick woman in Mark 5. Did *she* have any difficulty in knowing what to ask? Certainly not. Well, you might argue, she didn't really ask, she just came up behind Jesus and touched His clothes. Yes, but coming and touching were her ways of asking.

In Mark 5 the woman's asking was commensurate to her need. For twelve years she had suffered as much at the hands of primitive doctors as from her hemorrhage. Her life was intolerable. She was on her way to an early grave.

Then "she heard the reports about Jesus." I love that verse. "She heard the reports about Jesus." What reports? That whoever came to Him was healed! Look back or think back into the gospel records. When was anyone refused who came to Jesus for help of any kind? There was no one. Everyone who came received the help he asked for. Lepers were cleansed, blind eyes were made to see, demons were cast out and personalities restored. The lame walked, the deaf heard, the dead lived again.

This sick woman heard what Jesus had done and although her malady was not listed among the others, she was so desperate she decided within herself that if He could heal all those diseases, He could heal hers, too. *He* could do it. No one else. She was sure now, that *He was the one.* Her own desperate need drew her to Him, and if she could only get to Him, she would be well.

It was a glorious moment when I began to see that the power and authority of Jesus Christ were most often used when individuals, not crowds, asked for help. There were only a few whom He healed who did not ask personally. This too, shows His willingness and His knowledge of our needs.

What shall we ask for?

The simple answer is, *ask for what you need.*

3. *How Shall We Ask?*

What are your deep personal needs? Have you prayed about them? Have you asked the Person who can take care of them, to do it? Have you had your prayers answered? Or do you just grumble, and rebel, and blame other people?

Ask says Jesus, ask largely, that your joy may be full (John 16:24).

How shall you ask?

When we look at the sick woman the answer to this question is simple, too. Ask in His presence. Get close to the Lord Jesus. Touch Him. He is the answer. He is my answer and He is your answer. He Himself is the answer.

"If you live in Me—abide vitally united to Me—and My words remain in you *and* continue to live in your hearts, ask whatever you will and it shall be done for you" (John 15:7, Amplified).

What does "if you live in Me" mean? It means that all my desire is centered in the Person of Jesus Christ, and apart from Him nothing permanently influences the real me.

How shall you ask?

In the dramatic account of her conversion story in *The Burden Is Light* Eugenia Price prayed only two words over and over from the depths of her heart and He heard. "Oh, God! Oh, God! Oh, God!" Her heart was so heavy there was nothing else she could do but call on His Name. It is not the actual words we pray, it is the condition of our hearts when we pray that brings the answer. In her case, as in all others, He Himself was the answer.

4. *Desire*

This brings us to the third point, desire. The sick woman in Mark's story had only one desire. A desire which had been a tiny seed of hope, and which grew through the reports which she heard about the healing power of Jesus. She believed that if she could get past all the obstacles and reach His side, she would be healed. Her need and her desire carried her past the forbidding obstacles of custom which kept women at home, and especially sick ones, lest they contaminate others.

How great is your need?

How deep is your desire?

Will it bring you to His side? Will it carry you past all that keeps you from Him? Will you stop what you are doing now, and kneel at His feet, in His presence? He is there. Ask, seek, knock. There *is* Someone on the other side of the door, and He will open it and give you all that He is. Christ and all His gifts are yours.

". . . the proof of God's amazing love is this: that it was while we were sinners that Christ died for us. If God is for us, who can be against us? He that did not hesitate to spare His own Son but gave Him up for us all—can we not trust such a God to give us, with Him, everything else that we need?" (Romans 5:8; 8:31,32, Phillips)

5. *Point of Contact*

Now we come to the last of our five lessons on faith, the necessity of a "point of contact."

What is a point of contact?

It is that very moment when you reach out and touch the hem of Jesus' garment, and with the woman you know you are healed.

Does living faith always have a person as a "point of contact?" Didn't the woman say that if she could but touch His clothing she would be healed? Wasn't it Jesus' garment that she touched? Yes, but was it Jesus' garment that healed her? Wasn't it rather the Person of Jesus Christ, and the power He possessed? He realized this, and that was why He embarrassed her by saying, "Who touched me?"

She had to tell her whole story anyway before the whole crowd. But Jesus had a good reason for this. Knowing human nature, He wanted to save her from the bondage which "experiences" or "relics" can have over us. Being a woman myself, I know what she might have done. She might have gone home looking for more symptoms, and even finding them. And then she might have started out once more to find Jesus, this time with a small pair of scissors concealed in her pocket. She might have cut off a piece of his robe, so that she could touch it whenever she felt ill.

Jesus, loving her, and knowing the importance of a personal relationship, said to her, "Daughter." He said more, "Daughter, *your faith* [that is, your trust and confidence in Me springing from faith in God] has restored you to health" (Mark 5:34, Amplified.) He is the One we must all touch. Our hearts must climb that step of faith into His presence. He is already with us, and conscious of us. Climbing the step of faith is merely realizing that He is there.

If it is with another person that *you* can better climb the step to faith, and pray a faith-sized request, then you should plan to meet and pray with someone else.

This is where Matthew 18:19, 20 takes on fresh meaning. Certain things we seem to be able to ask for and receive when we are alone. Other things loom like great mountains, and we need the faith and prayer of one or two others to help us when we pray. "If two of you agree (harmonize together, together make a symphony) about— anything and everything—whatever they shall ask, *it will come to pass and be done* for them by My Father in heaven" (Amplified.)

Your point of contact is when you touch Jesus Christ, whether you are alone or with someone else. And your point of contact may be determined beforehand.

How does one find that point of contact? By asking, by praying, by being consciously with Him in prayer. Listen for His voice, the voice of the Shepherd who goes before His sheep. He will tell you. He is your first "point of contact." He will show you what to do next.

Our little sick woman in Mark's account had a point of contact, and who knows how long it had been in her heart? She would steal up behind him, so no one would be embarrassed by her illness, so she would not have to tell what it was, and reach her hand through the crowd that milled around Jesus. When she *touched His clothing* she would be healed. She knew it beforehand. That was her point of contact.

Your point of contact may be that very moment at which two of you agree in prayer. It may be the moment the other person lays his hand on your head or your shoulder and prays for you. It may be the moment you kneel at an altar of prayer. If you listen for the Shepherd's voice in your inner heart, He will tell you and He will lead you, and He will heal your heart or your body, for He is both able and willing.

Living faith is always in the Person of Jesus Christ. The Chinese word for faith, *hsin*, has several interesting root-characters. On the left side stands a man, on the right side is a small squarish opening out of which spring several short lines, denoting a mouth and the words being spoken. So then, faith is the confidence one has in a man and his words.

Do you believe in Jesus Christ? Then you have faith. Faith to ask Him for anything because you believe in Him. You will know what to ask and how and where, because you believe in Him and love Him. Your greatest need can be your greatest asset, for need is the golden door through which He comes close to His loved ones. Christ promised, "Lo, I am with you all the days,—perpetually, uniformly and on every occasion—to the [very] close and consummation of the age" (Matthew 28:20, Amplified.)

Jesus Christ is our "point of contact," and as we touch Him, alone or with others, power is released and our prayers are answered.

CHAPTER 9

WHAT IS UNANSWERED PRAYER?

In this chapter we will look at the difference between unanswered prayer and obstructed prayer.

Is there such a thing as unanswered prayer?

Some people seem to think so, because recently I found this quotation: "Many of our prayers are not answered, and for this we should be grateful." In one sense, that is true. But whoever wrote that was speaking of the foolish and unwise things we are apt to ask for in our human ignorance.

I am sure the Lord, in His great loving wisdom, sifts all our requests, and the ones which might harm us are not answered according to our asking. Because of His care over us, all that may seem disappointing will in the end be beneficial. I believe this, because I am learning more and more about what He is like. God is greater by far than any idea or concept man could possibly conceive in his little mortal mind.

However, there are prayers which are "unanswered" because they are hindered. They could be answered, and some day they may be answered, but for a time they are held up by some obstacle. The heavy snows in Chicago held up morning traffic this past winter for six hours. But when colliding cars were hauled away and the snow plow got through, the flow of traffic went on.

Is there a chief obstacle which may hinder our prayers? Jesus mentions lack of forgiveness a number of times in references closely connected with prayer promises. The text doesn't really state plainly that unforgiveness will keep our prayers from being answered, but it is strongly implied. Jesus says, "When you stand praying, forgive . . ." and, "If you do not forgive, neither will your heavenly Father forgive" (Mark 11:25, 26).

I'd like to mention three qualifying conditions for answered prayer in the gospel accounts. All of them are stated in the positive (but there is a negative meaning implied).

1. That we should ask in His Name (John 16:24).
2. That we should let His words live in our hearts (John 15:7).
3. That we should not be discouraged if we do not receive an immediate answer, but we should keep on asking, keep on knocking and keep on believing (Matthew 7:7, 8).

Let us examine the meaning of these three conditions.

1. *In His Name* means "presenting all I AM" (Amplified). All of the character of Jesus Christ is set forth in His Name. This means all of the character of God. What we ask, then, should be in keeping with what He is like, and a request unlike Him cannot be granted to us.

2. To let His words live, or abide in us, as a condition for answered prayer, means that we let Him live right in our hearts. Jesus Christ is Lord. *He contains His words.* This is a vital union of two hearts, the one living within the other. Such oneness would produce a unity of purpose. So how could one ask for anything that was not right and pure and good?

3. To have our prayers answered, we must keep on asking, keep on seeking, keep on knocking, for this is the continuing action of the Greek verb in Matthew 7:7,8 and also of Luke 11:5-13, the story of the man who wanted bread at midnight, and kept asking until he got it. Don't give up. Don't get discouraged, keep asking. Why? The only reason I know is that prayer changes me because I am in His presence, and then I either begin to change my requests, or I become able to cope with my circumstances which may or may not change.

So there are no unanswered prayers in one sense, because if we ask for what we want in His Name, and we are living in Him, and we keep on asking, the answer will come. It may be yes or it may be no, but God sends it, and it will be the best.

We do understand, however, that some answers to our prayers are delayed, and this is because God answers them in His way instead of in ours.

But hindered or obstructed prayer is a very real thing and is not the same as unanswered prayer. When we are not living in Chirst or letting Him live in us, there is always a reason. John, in his first epistle (I John 3:21,22) tells us that if our hearts are guilty because we are not watchfully observing His suggestions and plans for us, our guilty hearts will keep us from coming boldly to God. And our guilty hearts will keep us from asking and receiving what God wants to give us (Amplified).

This explains how unforgiveness or resentment toward another can hinder our prayers. Unforgiveness on our part automatically creates guilt in us. If I cannot love my brother whom I can see, how can I love God whom I cannot see? (I John 4:20) Love of God and love of our fellow man go together. *I will love God only as much as I love the person I dislike the most.* The kind of love God commands us to have is a genuine caring about what happens to the other person. It doesn't necessarily mean being attracted to him. It means caring about what happens to him.

As long as I am blinded by an unforgiving spirit toward my brother, how can I see God? There is blessedness for the pure in heart, for they see God. Lack of forgiveness is the equivalent of an impure heart. Resentment and unforgiveness are the roots of many diseases from which people suffer intensely. Only God can heal an unforgiving heart. Forgiveness is the ultimate proof of love, both of God's love and of our love to one another.

Love goes into action to make the first move. Love does not wait for the other person to come first. Love does not wait for the other person to take the blame and reach out first. These are some of the ways of love.

To be unforgiving is rebellion against God. He wants to forgive our sins, but Jesus says again and again that we must forgive others when we pray, so that our Father can forgive us our sins. To refuse to do this is rebellion. All rebellion is initially against God. All sin comes under that word, "rebellion." No matter what it is, it is some kind of self-assertion which is leaving God out. It is some kind of defiance, open or secret, which resists the authority of Jesus Christ in one's life.

Rebellion would be a real obstacle to having one's prayers answered, wouldn't it? And this is sin. And so there it is. Sin is the only thing which hinders one's prayers from being answered. And what will we do about that? What can we do? Confess our sins? Die to sin? Or carry with us a partial-condemnation all day long, day after day, because we are "not all that God wants us to be?"

I had a strong sense of rightness in going ahead with this chapter, because for many long impossible years I tried to be free from sin. I tried to die to sin. I tried to confess it all. I tried to believe it was all gone. Now, with great relief, I know I am a sinner *being* saved. I am not doing it myself. I have been saved, I am being saved, and I shall be saved. And He is doing it all. I know that Jesus Christ, by His death and by His life, is my righteousness.

I want to give you one of my favorite Bible verses on this subject, regarding what to do about sin in one's life. For me, this was the answer, and showed me how Jesus Christ is taking full responsibility for my life.

The Amplified New Testament is clear on Romans 5:10. "For if while we were enemies we were reconciled to God through the death of His Son, it is much more [certain], now that we are reconciled, that we shall be saved [daily delivered from sin's domination] through His [resurrection] life."

All the known or unknown rebellions of my life are being taken care of through the power of Jesus Christ's resurrected life. I know, too, that He expects me to cooperate with Him in bringing my will under His control, so that all these rebellions can be stripped of their dominating power. When, face to face, I am alone with Him in prayer, and His love is pouring over me, somehow it is possible to hand over to Him the specific thing that I wanted to manage myself.

And you, my tender-hearted, overly conscientious friend, can rest in Him, too, so that your prayers will be answered, and so that you do not need to continue condemning yourself.

Who is he that condemns? Do you know the answer to that question? Do you condemn yourself? Oh, yes, we do, in a way that helps us turn positively to Christ. But the morbid, negative daily condemnation which is sapping the life out of you, and keeping you from receiving all He wants to give you, is wrong. Because He has already died for you. The Christ who died for you and rose again is the only One who can condemn you. And He does not (Romans 8:31-39). He loves you. He loves you more than you are loved by anyone else in this world or in the next.

God loves you. The Son of Man is come not to condemn
but to save (John 3:17).

When you do find something that condemns you, bring
it at once to His feet, and it will be transformed. Because
all the fruits of the Spirit are sins transformed. Resentment
is changed to love. Sadness is changed to joy. Unbelief is
changed to faith. Rebellion is changed to acceptance.
These are simply the gifts which accompany the Giver.
Where He is, and where He lives, are all the good things
He wants to give to us. We don't pick faith out of the air,
or off a limb.

Jesus Christ is our faith.

There is, of course, the possibility that you don't want to
be changed in some area. That could really put an obstacle
in front of your prayers, and they might have to wait some
time for an answer. And yet, here again, God is so great
and His love so strong that He knows why we balk at
something, and He lets us sulk or pity ourselves, while He
in His eternal goodness keeps on giving and giving. And
who can question Him? Who can say what He should do
or what He shouldn't do? The fact remains,

> God loves all people.
>
> All people are sinners.
>
> Therefore God loves all sinners.

It is true no matter from what angle you approach it.
God loves you, as you are, in your rebellions, in your sins,
and He loves you eternally. The proof of this was a Man
on the cross, an historical fact, already more than nineteen
hundred years old and yet ever true. Because this Man
lives today!

> *God so loved . . . that He gave*
>
> *His only begotten son . . .*

*And he died for all, so that all those who live might
live no longer to and for themselves, but to and for
Him Who died and was raised again for their sake* (II
Corinthians 5:15, Amplified).

*Keep on asking and it will be given you; keep on
seeking and you will find; keep on knocking [rever-
ently] and the door will be opened to you. For
everyone who keeps on asking receives, and he who
keeps on seeking finds, and to him who keeps on
knocking it will be opened* (Matthew 7:7, 8 Amplified).

CHAPTER 10

WHAT ARE FAITH-SIZED REQUESTS?

What is a faith-sized request?

A faith-sized request is first of all a request which is just the right "believing" size for your faith. It is not a request which is so large that the very size of it makes you wonder if God will answer. It is a request for a particular situation, in which you pray for a special person or thing, and ask only for that which you can *really believe God will do*, in a given time limit. This does not limit what God can do, but it honestly recognizes the size of your faith. And there is every reason to believe that you will be asking for larger things as your faith grows.

Let me illustrate this by a prayer-promise in Mark and also by several true experiences.

> *Jesus ... said to them, Have faith in God (constantly). Truly, I tell you whoever says to this mountain, Be lifted up and thrown into the sea! and does not doubt at all in his heart, but believes that what he says will take place, it will be done for him.*
>
> *For this reason I am telling you, whatever you ask for in prayer, believe—trust and be confident—that it is granted to you, and you will [get it]* (Mark 11:22-24, Amplified).

The first thing the Lord tells us is to have faith in the One who is able to answer. That is one of the lessons in faith which we examined in Chapter 8. Then we are told that no matter what mountain stands in our way, if we *ask and believe it will be moved, it will be done*.

To ask and believe is the opposite of wondering in your heart if you will receive it. That negative picture in your mind of "not receiving" what you asked for is doubt, and doubt will surely keep your prayer from being answered. But God has given us power over our imaginations, so that by the positive use of that imagination, we can picture ourselves receiving the answer. This is the way to believe in one's heart, and to believe that what one has asked for, he will receive.

Jesus repeats this promise again in the next verse, and does not limit it to any one mountain. He says, "*Whatever* you ask for in prayer, believe ... that it is granted to you, and you will get it."

Those are strong, positive words. There is no "if" or "maybe" involved. Why is it then, that we don't ask for more? Why is it then, that we seem to get so little when so much is needed?

About the time I began to be aware of honesty and simplicity and brevity in audible prayer, I listened carefully when others prayed, and also checked myself after I had prayed. I asked myself these questions:

For what *definite* thing had I prayed?

Did I believe that I would get it?

Could I picture myself receiving it?

The tragic answer was, that I wasn't asking anything definite, and I wasn't receiving anything definite. I was merely praying platitudes, "Lord, bless my family in America, and bless the Chinese pastors working in Shanghai, and bless ... and bless ... and bless...." The words bless and blessing do get a workout when people pray! But what exactly are we asking for? Are we asking for anything? Are we talking to anyone? Are we expecting an answer from Him?

Two things began to appear in my short simplified prayers. I saw to it that I thanked Him for something, and I asked Him for something, no matter how small it seemed. It was hard to keep my prayers short at first, but I did it deliberately in order to make myself think specifically, and not just let words flow out without any thought back of them.

And in the asking, I was careful to ask only for that which I believed He could do. If you think it is easy, try it, and keep your mind on being definite. The first thing I knew, I was editing my prayers. I would ask for something, and then quickly ask for forgiveness, because I found I didn't really believe I would get what I was asking for. Then I'd try again and finally I would arrive at one small request (compared to the first one) which I confidently believed God could do and would do in the given situation.

In my book, *The Years That Count*, I have illustrated this point in a detailed story in the 17th chapter. When Karen prayed for the conversion of her boy friend, Chuck, she was unable to believe he would be saved the first week, but she was able to believe that, on the very next date, she could tell him about her own Saviour. She was enabled to do this. Then she prayed that he would accept a New Testament. He did. Then, that he would be willing to read it. He was willing. And the story goes on, until two weeks after her first request, Chuck made an open acknowledgment of faith in Jesus Christ.

It is too frequently our experience to pray for the conversion of a loved one for years without an answer. That is not because God isn't willing to save the loved one, it's because we are not praying sensibly and with faith. It is like trying to take one giant leap from the bottom of the stairs to the top of the stairs. We *want* to get to the top of the stairs. We talk and talk about going and yet there we stand. The reason being, it is impossible to get from the bottom to the top of a flight of stairs in one step. Stairs were made to be used, but they were made to be used one step at a time!

The prayer of faith is like that. Climbing the steps is what we mean by a faith-sized request. Take one step at a time. Pray for only what you believe God can do, for a certain person in a definite situation during a given time period.

To futher illustrate faith-sized requests, I'd like to give you the experience of a married couple who moved into a new neighborhood. One of the first requests Mary and Jack made was, "Lord, we'd like to get acquainted with our neighbors, and if they don't know You personally as their Saviour, we'd like to introduce them to You."

That was a fine request and right in line with what God wanted to do. But it was the description of a goal to be reached, not a step to take. They got down to business then, and took the first step.

"Lord," prayed Jack, "I'd like to meet the fellow living next door in some casual way and begin to get acquainted with him. I'd like to begin today, and I believe You can arrange it for me. Thank you, Lord." Mary agreed with Jack in her prayer, and gave thanks with Him.

The morning had scarcely turned to afternoon when the

answer came. Their children got into a quarrel over a tricycle with the neighbor's children. Both fathers rushed to the scene. Jack took all the blame for his children, and put out his hand, "I'm Jack M., just moved in, glad to meet you." The first request had been answered. The first step had been taken.

The second step: "Lord, I'd like to know what that man is interested in, so we could become friends." The answer came within two days. He was interested in football.

The third step: "Lord, I need two complimentary football tickets, and could I have them by this weekend, please." The tickets came. The friendship grew.

The fourth step: "Lord, I'd like to invite this new friend to the Bible class I teach a few miles from here. Would You put it into his heart to accept when I ask him to go with me tonight?" He accepted. All the way over as they drove, they talked about football. All the way home they talked about Jesus Christ, and what it meant for Him to become one of us . . . God became a Man.

The fifth step: "Lord, Mary and I would like to invite my friend and his wife to our home some evening this week and have a little talk and Bible reading together." The friends came, and they read and talked quietly together.

The sixth step. "Lord, next week when I ask them over again, will You prepare their hearts, so that they will be ready to accept You as their Saviour? I believe this is the time to ask for this, and I thank You for all You'll be doing in the meantime to draw them to Yourself." When the next week came, the neighbors willingly and gladly accepted Jesus Christ.

This method works also in matters of guidance about getting a job, taking a trip, buying or selling a house, getting married, writing a book, or anything you may think of yourself, small or large.

Here is another illustration. Last year at the Mound Keswick Conference in Minnesota, I met Rev. Harold De Vries, one of the speakers. We both attended each other's meetings. My subjects were conversational prayer and faith-sized requests.

After returning to his church Mr. De Vries spoke to his people about conversational prayer, and sometime later the women of the church invited me to speak to them on the same subject. Two months ago, Mr. De Vries told a friend something of what was happening among a few groups meeting to pray conversationally.

"Why wouldn't it be a good idea for your people to meet in small groups and learn to pray like this?" his friend asked.

Mr. De Vries decided he would introduce the subject at the next Wednesday night prayer meeting. During the day he asked the Lord to send 150 persons to prayer meeting that night. Then he remembered "faith-sized requests," and asked himself if he really believed God could send 150 people.

He changed his prayer. "Lord, I believe you can and will send one hundred interested persons to prayer meeting tonight."

There were one hundred persons there that night, and they were all interested in forming groups to pray conversationally. By the next Sunday another fifty had signed up, making a total of 150 who are meeting regularly in groups of from two to six in homes, in offices, in the suburbs and in the Loop. The needs of the people are being met. Spontaneous prayer is offered for one another, faith-sized requests are being answered, more people are taking part, requests are being covered. There are fewer clichés, less padding, more honesty and simplicity in prayer. Men and women are coming close to God and to each other in the Winnetka Bible Church.

The wonderfully exciting thing about faith-sized requests when two or more are praying is that so many times as you pray by subjects, exactly the same request will come to two or more of you at the same time. That is when *faith* rejoices and cries, "It shall be done!" That is the moment when doubt disappears. That is when the whole mountain moves—or sometimes only half of it. But the other half will go, too, if you are willing to wait for the next step.

CHAPTER 11

WHEN PEOPLE PRAY TOGETHER

The book, *Prayer Can Change Your Life*, by Dr. William R. Parker (Prentice-Hall) is the story of an unusual experiment which applies the methods of modern psychology to the study of prayer.

By the use of three controlled groups, Dr. Parker and his co-author, Elaine St. Johns, were attempting to find out if prayers, rightly understood and practiced, would equal the treatment of psychotherapy.

For this purpose forty-five volunteers were interviewed and carefully divided into three groups of fifteen individuals each.

Group 1 was to be given the best psychotherapy possible in weekly individual counseling sessions for the purpose of remedying emotional disorders.

Group 2 was made up of the random pray-ers, who preferred neither the psychotherapy nor the prayer therapy. They were to pray alone every night during the nine months.

Group 3, the prayer therapy group, was to meet weekly for a two-hour session to talk and pray together.

All forty-five were given five recognized personality tests to determine what lay in the subconscious that might be a clue to the problems and disturbances in each life. The findings were also to act as a guide to determine progress at the end of the nine months.

In the prayer therapy group, a sealed envelope was handed to each individual once a week, which contained his homework. On this slip was written some undesirable emotion, discovered through the tests, about which he was to pray earnestly for that one week; the next week he was told to forget about that one, and was given another envelope and another piece of homework. There was no suggestion made that the contents should be shared, but soon the group voluntarily began discussing and sharing their own experiences and the progress they were making.

Dr. Parker reports that *inhibitions and barriers crumbled as they recognized that each one needed the help and the healing and encouragement that came from sharing with the group.*

At the end of nine months, the tests revealed the following results:

Group 1. Those receiving individual psychotherapy with no mention of religion or prayer, showed 65% improvement, but each desired more treatment during the coming months.

Group 2. The random pray-ers, who prayed every night on their own showed no improvement at all.

Group 3. The prayer therapy group showed 72% improvement both in symptoms and tests, and the conclusive evidence of spiritual healing was indicated by the fact that *all of them wanted to help others as they had been helped.*

If you feel you need to be in a prayer group of this kind, you do not necessarily need to be in a controlled group such as Dr. Parker conducted. The story of what happened to the fifteen persons in the prayer therapy group has happened to many other groups who met and prayed with simplicity and honesty. It can happen to you and to your group. It isn't necessary that some certain person give you special lessons on conversational prayer.

It is necessary only that you thoroughly believe in the therapy of group prayer, as taught by Jesus Christ in Matthew 18:19, 20.

There are no formal or rigid rules for conducting any prayer group. We come together first of all to pray, and to be conscious that we are in the presence of God, where we find spiritual hope and healing for all the ills of body, mind and spirit.

1. *How to Start a Prayer Group*

If you are *not* now connected with any group, and want to pray with someone, *ask* as the Lord Jesus has commanded. "Ask, and you shall receive." Start with one person. Send a copy of this book to a friend whose name will come to you when you pray. Find out later how he or she liked it, and suggest that you two meet together to pray. It is the Father who has made us members of His family, and it is His will that we find each other and learn to talk to Him together.

If you *are* connected with some group, share with one or two of the members your own personal prayer failures. Do this without blaming anyone else, and then discuss the remedy which you believe will be helpful. Share this book or another book on prayer. Read it aloud together, and discuss it honestly, and then stop and pray together right there. New habits will have to be formed and old ones broken. This takes practice and concentration. Prayer's function is to set God at the center of your attention, and forget yourself and the impression you are making on others. As you open your own heart (saying *I*, when you mean yourself, and *we*, when you mean all of those present) you will find God's love and joy healing the old hurt places.

2. *The Place*

Because this is an informal kind of prayer, the place too, should be informal. Not a large room or auditorium. Unless you can arrange the chairs in a circle in one corner, a small room is always better. It should be a place where you will be undisturbed. Any possibility of disturbance will tend to check the ease and freedom of those praying, and interrupt the line of thought. If your children are screaming in the basement, you are probably used to it by this time, but someone else may not be. Pray about the location and the right answer will come.

3. *The Size of the Group*

The Michigan church about which I wrote in Chapter 6 started their prayer meeting with twelve, with the idea of dividing as the group grows. Since they are new at praying aloud, it is better for them to stay together until a real love and union of hearts has been reached through conversing with God. Then as their hearts are open to Him who speaks to hearts, they will know when and how they should divide.

In the Winnetka Bible Church (Chapter 10) their groups range from two to six.

In Lima, Ohio, a large group meets in a home, and after sharing and Bible study, groups of four and five go into almost every room in the house to pray.

When the group is small, the members feel free to pray as often as they need to. If the group is too large, someone is sure to use it as an excuse to say to himself, "It doesn't matter if I don't pray, the others will." Small groups may upon occasion pray together as a large group. But the strength of any large group is in the smaller intimate prayer groups who meet God face to face.

4. The Time

Any time is the time for group praying. Any time when two people can get together. A telephone conversation is a wonderful time to pray; you may feel self-conscious at first but that will soon go.

The length of the prayer meeting will vary and will be determined, each time, by the needs of the group. I know of one group of young people which spent most of the forty-five minutes in singing, reading Scripture, giving requests, with only about five or ten minutes for actual praying. After conversational prayer was introduced, they reversed the program. Actually, this group of teenagers prayed one and a half hours the first time they tried praying conversationally. They could scarely believe it! They had enjoyed every minute and wanted more. That was because all of them were praying all the time.

5. The Position

Sitting around the table draws people together in an easy yet intimate way. Sitting in a circle is also a favored position. Or kneeling by a sofa, or at an altar. Scattered seating is to be avoided. We are members of one family. And remember, don't pray into a sofa or a chair so no one can hear.

6. How to Make an Actual Beginning

a. Explain to your group what conversational prayer is, and why you want to pray this way.

b. Always remind yourselves, by a time of silence first, that you are actually in the presence of Jesus Christ. Act accordingly and prepare your heart in quiet worship. Don't be afraid of silence. He is there, and He speaks in a still small voice.

c. Then let someone open with a prayer of thanks that Matthew 18:19, 20 is true. (That He is there with you. You have recognized His presence in your individual hearts in silence.)

d. Let others give thanks also, in sentence prayers. Give thanks first of all for the Lord Himself, for what He is like, for Himself alone. Then for His gifts: for eternal life, for some personal answer to prayer.

e. Let the "asking" or requests wait until everyone has joined one or more times in the thanksgiving. This may take a little reminding, as many people do not distinguish between worship and requests, between the Giver and the gifts.

7. Giving Requests

Stating prayer requests to the group before you start to pray can be a time-consuming and evasive practice. I well remember a meeting when the giving of requests lasted three times longer than the actual praying. It apparently is much easier to tell our problems to one another than to God.

The familiar "unspoken requests" can also be evasive, and tend to draw the person who gave them farther off into his or her lonely position.

As members of God's family (and members of the body of Christ) we are told to "bear one another's burdens." How can we do this unless we know the burdens others are carrying, and unless we make known our own burdens? "Bearing our own burden" could mean that the person who has the request upon his mind is the one who is to do the initial praying. Norman Grubb says that the man who has a definite desire or need is the man who has the faith to do the asking.

As soon as one has prayed about his own burden, another in the group should pick it up and pray, too, mentioning the person by name. This is what we mean when we say, "praying by subjects" (Chapter 3). Let as many as feel led by the Holy Spirit pray for this person until he or she is able to give thanks, or until there is freedom for someone else to introduce a new subject of prayer.

8. Agreeing in Prayer

Matthew 18:19, 20 tells us to agree in prayer and we shall have an answer. How do we know when we have agreed?

Take the situation mentioned above. The person who

made his difficulty known needs help. He may need some definite help. What is the next step he should take? Always ask yourself and ask the Lord, too: *What is the next step?*

When we pray together the Holy Spirit speaks to our hearts and suggests ways and means. When we are quiet and aware that we are in His presence, we are exercising love for one another. The "tree prayer meeting" in Chapter 3 is a good example of this kind of praying, but that is such a brief example. I've seen members of a group bear someone's burden until the same answer "was given" to several at the same time! And there was fullness of joy, just as Jesus Christ promised in John 16:24.

We agree that God's will be done. We agree by saying so when we pray. We agree that our brother will know the next step, even if it is doing nothing. Even if it is just waiting.

People who meet in small groups to pray usually begin to know each other well. We do not need to explain things to God in prayer (because He knows everything) unless it will help relieve our minds. We may come with confidence and ask with confidence. If you need to explain things to each other, stop praying for a moment and do the explaining. Conversational praying is very natural, so whatever comes up, keep things natural.

When we don't know *what* to agree about, that is when the group goes into real Spirit-filled love action. We remind the Lord of His promises, we hold our brother's situation up in prayer, we mention his name, we lift together (each member perhaps doing one of these things). With our minds set together in this way, we break through whatever darkness there is, or move whatever mountain may be in the way. This we do and believe we can do because Jesus Christ is present with us, and because we are asking in His nature, in His character and in His will. Asking in His Name means all of these things. We converse in prayer, we suggest, we wait, we break in, we become aware, we stay in tune. (Conversation is defined in Chapter 3.)

9. *The Leader*

This subject was purposely left until number 9, so that no undue emphasis might be put upon it. He or she is only a chairman, or a moderator, not really a "leader" at all. He should be sensitive, aware of the moving of the Spirit in the group, and of the brother or sister who needs that extra lift, which he can give by praying for him. As he feels moved by the Spirit, he can suggest various prayer subjects, examples of which will be listed in the next paragraph. However, don't ever feel that you must cover all of these in one meeting. It is the work of the Spirit to guide. And it is a life changing experience to see how He does this through the honest spoken needs of various members of the group.

10. *Prayer Subjects*

Worship, thanksgiving, praise to God: the Father, the Son and the Holy Spirit.

Prayer for our loved ones.

Prayer for our own personal needs or projects.

Prayer for each other (i.e., ask each one to pray for the person to his right or left).

Prayer for your pastor and your church.

Prayer for those involved in a current newspaper account of a tragedy, etc.

Prayer for our nation, our statesmen, our missionaries.

11. *Silence—Pauses*

Someone has said, "Right prayer demands a quieting of the whole being." We need to learn to be quiet, and to be consciously aware of Jesus Christ. We cannot pray quietly if we are in a hurry to get going again. It is in the silences, between prayers, that He speaks to us, and that our communion with Him purges and renews us. We should give audible thanks after such a time of silence. When no one is praying audibly, all should be praying silently, and should be so instructed. We are not there primarily to "get things" but to realize God's presence. This is the greatest answer to prayer, that we are consciously aware of the Great Shepherd and His unchanging love for us.

12. *Honesty as We Pray*

If no one in the group is willing to be honest, there will soon be no prayer meeting.

The principle of honesty in prayer is twofold: First, that I say *I,* when I mean myself, and that I say *we* when I include the whole group. The editorial *we* denotes the deadly poison of dishonesty. Here is one version: "Lord, we ought to pray more often, and we ought to read our Bibles more often, forgive us." Here is the other: "Lord, forgive me. I've read my Bible only once or twice this week, and I've just prayed on-the-run, and my heart is so hungry to be with You alone. Please forgive me for this, and I put the controls of my day back into Your hands."

The second principle of honesty is to pray where I am and not where I am not.

If I am struggling over hurt feelings for instance, I should say so, and do it without involving or blaming anyone but myself. It is dishonest to pray as though everything were fine and shining when that isn't true. If the matter is too personal to mention, you can still be honest enough to ask for strength to face a decision, or for grace to help in a certain situation. It has been said that "one gets it off one's chest by getting it on one's tongue." (See I John 1:9.) Honesty demands straightforward simplicity without apology.

Honesty goes right to the point.

13. *Difficulties*

a. *If one person prays too often.* I know from my own experience how eager one can become. Fortunately a friend took me aside and told me. "Wouldn't it be better if you waited a bit, to see if the Spirit might place the same request or the same answer upon someone else's heart? Then you would have the joy of knowing that both of you were agreeing in the Spirit." It *was* much better. I became more aware of the need of others to express themselves, to take part in agreeing and thus fulfill the royal law: love one another.

b. *If one or more persons insist on long prayers.* This demands love and instruction. Perhaps first to the whole group, and then to the individual. Perhaps he or she will begin to pray shorter prayers as you pray and God answers. Long prayers tend to become impersonal and indirect, and when the group is praying conversationally, the others feel left out and unable to participate.

Try suggesting sentence prayers, or enough sentences to convey one idea only. If the person is new, someone should clue him in before starting.

c. *If one is praying an honest prayer*. Then you be that one. It will hurt. It may kill you. Kill your pride, that is. But it will bring rich abundant life. When God meets *you* in your honesty, someone else will realize a deep heart hunger to meet Him in the same way.

When the Holy Spirit is in full charge, there will be real freedom to pray honestly, and sins will be forgiven and tensions will be released. The natural and expected result of prayer, in the Presence of God, is that healing love shall touch us all as we sit in our places.

After all, prayer is conversing with God, and to converse with someone we must be with that person.

And in His presence is fullness of joy.

APPENDIX

1. DAILY QUIET TIME
   A three-day devotional study for new believers.

2. AIDS TO PERSONAL WORSHIP
   A seven-day devotional in the art of meditation and worship.

3. A DIAGRAM OF THE TRINITY

4. HEART-SEARCHING SCRIPTURES
   A two-hour personal meditation.

DAILY QUIET TIME

Purpose: The following pages contain a sample Quiet Time for those who have never settled down to a daily, regular devotional time, and who wish to make this a part of their Christian lives. May be used for retreats, etc. Any age.

Suggestions: If you wish to do this three-day study, read again the four pointers for the Quiet Time in the first half of Chapter 7. Read only today's lesson. Keep each day's material fresh for the day on which you wish to use it.

Time: About twenty minutes for each study.

History: These three devotional studies were originally used at weekend conferences for young people ranging in age from sixteen to twenty-five. The pages were handed to the cabin counselor, who then made personal contact with each one during the day, as a follow-up procedure.

First Day

I. MEETING WITH GOD

Meditation: Bring your thoughts to Jesus Christ.

My Purpose: To meet Jesus Christ, my living Lord.
To be quiet, and put all other thoughts out of my mind.
To say to myself, *He is here.*
To welcome Him, and to be glad.

II. TALKING WITH GOD

Prayer. Use these thoughts to make your own prayers. Time 5 minutes.

1. To give thanks means: To be grateful. Think of all you have to be grateful for, in your past, in your present. For the knowledge of God, of Jesus Christ, of the Holy Spirit. Be grateful for the Giver as well as His gifts.

2. To give thanks: For the pleasant things and the things that hurt you and cause you to suffer. Jesus suffered for us. He knows. Give thanks.

III. LETTING HIM TALK TO ME

Bible reading: Time 15 minutes.

My opening prayer. Psalm 119:18. Memorize it.

1. John 1:1-18. Study verses by reading more than once.
Read quietly, think of the meaning.
Read it again, aloud, to yourself.

2. John 1:1-14. For specific study.
   a. Who is "the Word"? ....
   b. Write out verses 2, 3, 4, and put the name you wrote above in place of the pronoun "he" or "him." If you have the right name, this will make good sense.
   c. Who made the world and all of us? ....
   d. Make a list of the other names by which He is called in verses 1-18.

IV. QUESTIONS

Yes   No

1. Can one inherit Christ from one's parents?

    ....

2. Do you have a friend who is a real
   Christian?   ------   ------

3. Have you ever definitely accepted
   Christ as your Saviour?   ------   ------
   When and where? ....

Second Day

I. MEETING WITH GOD

   Meditation: Time 3 minutes.

   My Purpose: To meet God face to face and worship
                    Him.
                    To give thanks and learn to worship.
                    To learn to be quiet and alone with
                    Him.

II. TALKING WITH GOD

   Prayer: Make your own prayers including the above
   thoughts, as well as the following:

   Time: 5 minutes.

   1. To worship God: Worship means that honor and
      respect and attitude of adoration that a small earth-
      ling like me can feel and give to the Great Al-
      mighty Creator, who is God and Saviour.

   2. Think on the above sentence. Break it down, think
      on the meaning of each word, each phrase. Then
      remember He wants your worship (John 4:23, 24),
      and start over again, and give it to Him, conscious-
      ly being aware that He is there. Use words and use
      thoughts in your heart which you can't even put
      into words. Worship the living God who loves you.

III. LETTING HIM TALK TO ME

   Bible reading: Time 15 minutes.

   Prayer: Psalm 119:18. Pray it.

   1. John 1:19-51. Give thanks for all you learned yes-
      terday about "The Word." Ask to be taught by the
      Holy Spirit today.

   2. Read aloud all of these verses. Time yourself, read
      slowly, and think of the meaning.
      How long did it take you? ....

   3. On the sheet you used yesterday, continue the

list of names used in this chapter for Jesus. How many do you have now? ....

IV. QUESTIONS

1. Do you think that Jesus Christ is God? ....

2. Why? Write your answer. ....
....
....
....

3. What made these disciples believe on Him? Write your answer ....
....
....
....

Third Day

I. MEETING WITH GOD

Meditation: Bring your thoughts to Jesus Christ. Be consciously in His presence.

My Purpose: To worship Him
To thank Him.
To let Him speak to me.
(Use thoughts of the other lessons.)

II. TALKING WITH GOD

1. To confess my own sins and needs in simple everyday language, and to accept and thank Him for His forgiveness and new life.

2. To pray for others: my friends and my family. He loves and cares for them, too.

III. LETTING HIM TALK TO ME

Bible reading: Time 15 minutes.

Prayer: Psalm 119:18. Pray it.

1. I John, chapters 1 and 2. Read these short chapters aloud.

2. Make a list of all the things you can find in these chapters that Christians should do.

3. Make a list of all the things Jesus Christ does for "little children" who belong to Him.

IV. QUESTIONS

Write down some of the things you have liked about this three-day meditation, the things which have helped you most.

Further Suggestions:

Read the helps for Daily Quiet Time given in Chapter 7. Take your hymn book with you into your Quiet Time, and meditate and think upon the words which inspired the writers: "When I Survey the Wondrous Cross," "What a Friend We Have in Jesus," etc.

AIDS TO PERSONAL WORSHIP

Purpose: A seven-day devotional study designed to lay a foundation in personal worship, through the study of some of the characteristics (or attributes) of God. The material is cumulative and progressive. Each day you will be using what you learned the day before.

Suggestions: It will be well to refresh your mind regarding the meaning of worship, by reading again the last half of Chapter 7.

Use the Introductory Lesson, as your first study. Please do not read tomorrow's lesson. Keep each lesson fresh for that day. Please try carefully and slowly to follow all instructions in order to gain the maximum good. These you will find sometimes so simple that only by doing them can you understand why they are of any value.

History: Aids to Personal Worship was originally prepared in a small mimeographed booklet, and used in month-long camps, first for teenagers, and subsequently for adults. The material has been tested and proven of inestimable value in teaching personal worship.

Introductory Lesson

1. My motive: To meet Jesus Christ, my living Lord.
2. My preparation: Each night as you drop off to sleep, pray that you may awaken with real expectation and readiness to arise and spend the first freshness of the day with Him.
3. The place: Find a place to be by yourself, where your face is toward Him alone. This is important.
4. The books: Try one of the newer, modern translations of the Bible, as well as your favorite Bible. Take a hymn book with you.
5. Learn to use the hymn book as a means of worship. The hymns you do not know will become familiar friends as you read through the verses and worship your Lord.
6. Apart from the fixed and resolute determination of your will to meet Him, you will find it impossible to do this daily. Your will, mind, heart and body are involved in worship.

MEDITATION:

True worship is subjection to Jesus Christ.

Our Lord seeks worshipers (John 4:23). True worship comes from those who are His sons. Let us worship whether we feel like it or not. Christ is worthy to be praised for WHO HE IS, and for what He has done, and for what He is doing.

DEFINITIONS FOR DEVOTIONAL STUDY

Worship . . . That honor, respect and adoration a small earthling· like me can feel and give to the Almighty Creator.

Praise . . . to glorify God in worship. To speak and sing of His Person, and of His works. To give thanks.

Glorify . . . to make wonderful and great by the love and devotion of my whole self to . . . God.

Confession . . . to be willing to face honestly my own sins and sinfulness, and put it into words.

Petition . . . to ask the Lord for whatever I need for myself.

Intercession . . . to pray for others, as I pray for myself.

Meditation . . . to think quietly about the Lord, turning over in my mind what I am reading, and letting it sink in.

Thanksgiving . . . to be grateful and show it. Not only for the gift received, but for the Giver. Be grateful and be thankful.

＊　　＊　　＊　　＊　　＊

"Come to me . . . Learn of Me."

First Day

MEDITATION

1. Enter His presence with expectation. "I am going to see Him, to meet Him!"

2. Humbly prostrate yourself. "He is the Great God, I am His child!"

3. Words are not necessary all the time. Just these silent thoughts and others like them. Take one of these, repeat it over and over until the full meaning begins to take hold of you.

"He is the great Eternal yet I can approach Him."

4. Wait. Be silent. Be reverent. Keep your mind on the above thoughts. Draw near remembering the blood of Jesus Christ, His Son, makes you clean.

HYMN

"Great Is Thy Faithfulness"

1. Read it. Sing it aloud. Choose another on the same subject if this one is not in your hymnal. Find out what it says about Him.

2. Select one verse. Underline the parts which describe our God.

3. Compare His faithfulness with yours. Confess your need.

4. Give thanks and praise to Him, now. Use the words of this hymn. Praise Him.

BIBLE READING

Ask the Holy Spirit to open your heart.
Memorize Psalm 119:18.

Read	Names of God	His Characteristics
1. Numbers 23:19		
2. James 1:17		
3. Hebrews 13:8		
4. Deuteronomy 7:9		
5. Psalms 145:13		
146:5, 6		
6. Psalm 91:4		

TESTING

The following words describe the central truth I learned about our God in this lesson.

PRACTICAL

Take with you all day these words and the ideas they convey. Recall them as many times as you can, with thanksgiving. This God is with you. Always. He loves you.

*   *   *   *   *

Real worship depends upon the kind of God you worship.

Second Day

MEDITATION

1. Using the instructions of yesterday, wait in His presence . . . until your heart and mind are very quiet. Quiet. Very quiet.

2. Remember . . . praise and worship belong to our God. (Review your definitions p. 80.)

HYMN

"Holy, Holy, Holy"

1. Sing it with your whole heart . . . remembering you are there before Him . . . offering your worship in song, in truth. Before His holiness I realize my unfitness . . . seeing Him, I am aware of my need. Yet He bids me come . . . He accepts me because He is one with God.

BIBLE READING

My prayer: Psalm 119:18.

1. Read Psalm 46. Go through it again, aloud.

2. Read it as though the whole world is listening and you are proud to belong to such a God.

> Pause to give thanks again.
> Pause to confess your own sinfulness
> before His pure holiness.

3. Turn to the Book of Revelation. Read of the holiness of Christ. Take your place . . . in imagination with the great throng and sing with them.

   Read the descriptive parts silently, and read the *praise* and *adoration* aloud.

Revelation 1:5-7)	Keep
Revelation 4)	your attention
Revelation 5)	upon the Lamb.

TESTING

From your reading today, write down the words that describe the Lord, your God: ....
....

PRACTICAL

1. *Give* thanks that through the Cross and Resurrection of Jesus Christ, you are made right . . . in His sight . . . that His holiness is yours for today's needs. He is your holiness.

2. *Share* with one person today what your Quiet Times so far have meant to you. Be specific.

*   *   *   *   *

Accept yourself as being sinful. To meet God is to cry out, "Depart from me, for I am a sinful man!" To meet God is also to cry out, "Thank you, LORD, because You have already taken full responsibility for me and my sin — forever!"

Third Day

MEDITATION

1. Enter His presence . . . with PRAISE. He loves you. He wants to let His love pour over you . . . like warm sunshine. Open . . . open and just rest. Rest and wait in His dear presence. Use the ideas (and notes) of the past two days.

2. On your knees. Call Him by all the names with which you are familiar. Repeat them . . . with love and adoration.

3. Let your WORSHIP be sometimes *silent,* with your whole being just going out toward Him; sometimes *vocal,* with just broken phrases, half-sentences, repeating His Name . . . for He is worthy.

4. Spend five or ten minutes in meditation. Do not leave until His love has warmed you, touched you, transformed you. Remember, HE LOVES YOU. His love meant . . . His death.

HYMN

Choose one of these, or a similar one:
"The King of Love"
"Jesus, I Am Resting"
"O Love That Wilt Not Let Me Go"
Read it, sing it, think of the meaning.
Underline the words describing His love.
Try "praying through" tne words, making them your prayer while you are singing.

BIBLE READING

1. Write out Romans 5:8: --

Circle tne important words. Pause to thank God for the real revelation of Himself in the wonderfu. Person of our Lord Jesus Christ.

2. I John 4:7-21. Read these verses. Form the habit of
   reading alone and aloud. Try it now.
   What word is repeated here? How many times?
   Meditate on the source of love . . . the progression . . .
   from whom to whom.
   List the characteristics of love, as found in God:
   ....; as found in you: ....

TESTING

Is there any person you will meet today to whom you
can show the kind of love Jesus showed on Calvary? With
forgiveness and gentleness, pray for him now. Love him
. . . now. Seek him out today. Show LOVE.

*   *   *   *   *

The first step in worship is learning to be alone with
God.

Fourth Day

MEDITATION

1. Combine the ideas of the first three days by writing
   down the phrases of praise and the names of the Lord
   from the hymns and Scriptures which you may remember.
2. Draw near . . . and let your whole being desire His
   presence. See how many of the things you have written
   can be recalled and quoted without looking.
3. Ask the Holy Spirit to teach you the real meaning of
   worship. Just ask Him . . . as you remember the words
   you have written.

HYMN

Choose a hymn, or select one of the following:
   "O Sacred Head, Now Wounded"
   "When I Survey the Wondrous Cross"
   "Hallelujah, What a Saviour!"

1. Read it aloud, slowly. Pray and praise with the author.
   Visualize the word pictures.
2. Find a few new expressions from this hymn to add to
   your growing list of praises with which you may adore
   your Lord.

BIBLE READING

1. Isaiah 53. Keep in mind that all this suffering was because He loves you.

Read the chapter, remembering the phrase from the hymn, "Thou hast loved us unto blood."

2. Read Isaiah 53 again, aloud. Have you learned to pray and read aloud yet? Our living Lord is there with you. Speak to Him. Share with Him.

   This suffering Saviour of Isaiah 53 is the same glorious Lamb of God who receives our praises in the Book of Revelation.

PRACTICAL

Spend some time in prayer today. Your growing love for your Lord means more love shown to your fellow man.

PRAY for your daily companions by name.

PRAY for members of your family by name.

PRAY for those you work with by name.

PRAY as the Holy Spirit leads you.

* * * * *

WORSHIP is meeting the living God and having my life changed by His presence.

Fifth Day

MEDITATION

Enter His presence with anticipation and praise.

He is here.

Worship Him in spirit and truth.

He is faithful, never-changing.

Holy, holy, holy! Lord God of Hosts!

Loving, faithful, Holy God! My Lord!

> *Lamb of God, my soul adores Thee,*
> *While upon thy face I gaze.*
> *Here the Father's love and glory*
> *Shine in all their brightest rays.*

Pause. Wait. Be still. Think on the meaning of each of the above words as you say them.

Use parts of other hymns to voice your praise.

HYMN

Choose a resurrection hymn, perhaps one of these:
   "Thine Be the Glory, Risen, Conquering Son"
   "Christ the Lord Is Risen, Today"

1. Notice to whom the hymn is addressed. Read it aloud.
2. Sing it, learn it if it is new.
3. Worship the Lord with this hymn.

BIBLE READING

1. John 19:19-31. Read it and see our Lord Jesus as the disciples saw Him at that time.

2. Psalm 33. Observe carefully all that He has done by His great, great power.

PRACTICAL

1. Make Psalm 33:18-22 your own prayer, by rewording the pronouns. Use the first person. "Behold, the eye of the Lord is upon *me*." Read it several times like this, adding your own requests, and enlarging them as the Holy Spirit puts them into your heart.

2. All your personal private prayer should be in the first person. We are talking to One who is a Person, and One who is alive forevermore.

PRAYER

For others by name.

Share today's plans with your Lord, and talk over all the details with Him.

* * * * *

Worship is the response of my whole self to God.

Sixth Day

MEDITATION

Spend at least 10 minutes, including the hymn, in meditation. By this time you have many ways to worship your Lord.

Confess your coldness (when you feel that way), for this is being honest as you pray.

"Come to me . . . learn of me . . . and ye shall find rest.

Let your heart pour out its silent gratefulness.

> From the world of sin and noise,
>   And hurry I withdraw;
> For the small and inward voice
>   I wait with humble awe;
> Silent am I now and still,
>   Dare not in Thy presence move;
> To my waiting soul reveal
>   The secret of Thy love.
>   —CHARLES WESLEY

HYMN

Choose one yourself for today. Choose one which expresses praise and worship to Christ.

BIBLE READING

Ephesians 1:15-2:10

Yesterday we read and thought about the power of our God, in creation, in becoming a man, in the resurrection. Today we want to see how that power operates in us, what that power does to us and in us.

Write what you find:

God's power in Christ   *God's power in us*

PRAYER

As your conception of the greatness of our God grows, your faith will reach out in prayer for your friends. Pray for them by name.

* * * * *

... the immeasurable greatness of His Power in us who believe.

... the immeasurable riches of His grace in kindness toward us in Christ Jesus."

Seventh Day

MEDITATION

Your meditation will usually consist of one or all of these

WORSHIP ... out of which proceeds

> PRAISE
>> CONFESSION
>>> PETITION
>>>> INTERCESSION
>>>>> THANKSGIVING

My voice shalt thou hear betimes, O Lord:
> Early in the morning
>> Will I order my prayer unto Thee
>> And will keep watch.

HYMN

Choose your own hymn.
Why did you choose it?
What did you find in it?

BIBLE READING

Psalm 139

First Reading: To get the general meaning and to open my heart for instruction by the Holy Spirit (John 14:26; 15-12-15).

Second Reading: To notice all that is said about me, and God's knowledge of me.

Third Reading: List all the characteristics of the Lord God as stated or implied in this psalm.

PRAYER

Be honest to the last detail.

This is the key which restores and maintains real fellowship between my Lord and me. Treat yourself to the luxury of real honesty in prayer. He knows it anyway, but He longs for you to be honest, for then you can hear Him speak to you. Have you learned to recognize His voice? (Proverbs 8:32-36; John 10:3, 4)

* * * * *

True worship is subjection to Jesus Christ.

A Diagram of the Trinity
See Page 27

HEART-SEARCHING SCRIPTURES

History: This meditation has been used in many weekend conferences and one-day workshops for groups ranging in size from 10 to 50.

Purpose: The Scriptures and the methods used are designed to help each one face afresh the "sin-question" in their own lives, as well as God's holiness, and the life Christ has promised for His children. Dullness in the Christian life is usually due to a "dim view" of sin, and this meditation is intended to help each one face up to specific "blocks" in his or her life, and to do something about them.

Suggestions: Start with the whole group. Use an appropriate hymn, and explain the purpose for the hour spent alone. Be sure everyone has a Bible, pencil and paper. Read the entire page aloud with the group, and ask if there are any questions.

After the hour alone, reassemble the group without unnecessary talking, and spend about a half hour in prayer, talking to the Lord Jesus about what He has shown, and thanking Him for what has been learned. Hymns of thanksgiving should be included in this period.

> "Create in me a clean heart, O God; and renew a right spirit within me" (Psalm 51:10).

A. HEART-SEARCHING SCRIPTURES

Romans 1:28-32	Matthew 23:25-28
Galatians 5:16-21	Colossians 3:8-15
II Timothy 3:1-5	Mark 12:28-31

1. Read slowly and thoroughly, over and over, the passages listed above. Read them prayerfully, until the Holy Spirit turns His light upon the present condition of your heart.

2. *Write down a list* of sins, shortcomings, failures as revealed . . . both in deed and in thought. Open your heart to a sense of the blackness of sin in God's holy presence, until He brings to you a deep sorrow which leads to true repentance. This will surely come if you wait for it. A definition of sin: My right to myself, my

natural independence and my self-assertiveness (Isaiah 53:6).

3. *Recognize and confess* sin, and don't be afraid to put it into words. If I take the easy way "Help me, Lord," my "worrying" (for instance) will continue with me the rest of my life! If I am honest, "Forgive this sin . . . against You, Lord . . . that I am not trusting You . . ." then the power of the Cross, and the Resurrection of the Lord Jesus are for me (I John 1:9).

4. *Ask yourself* these questions, and answer them:

   a. Is my sin against God? What attitude is back of this? What place have I given the Lord Jesus?

   b. Why have I been like this? What do I really want?

   c. What persons have I sinned against? (Matthew 5: 23, 24).

   d. Should I seek help with some of the things which I cannot forget and overcome alone?

B. WHAT CHRIST HAS DONE.   LIFE HE WILL GIVE YOU.

Hebrews 2:5-18	Psalm 32
Hebrews 10:12-18	John 4:14; 8:34-36
Hebrews 4:11-15	Psalm 103:1-4
	Ephesians 5:26, 27

With the use of a familiar hymn, meditate on the suffering and cost to Christ.

Remember that the Lord Jesus Christ is present there with you, and that you are in His presence. Be specific. Be honest. His forgiveness is for those who *come to Him*, those who will humble themselves before Him. He will meet you.

Remember, also, that the Heart-Searching Scripture study is primarily to help you find and face your subconscious barriers.

The Good News (Gospel) is not primarily, "confess, be honest, face up and God will forgive your sins." He will do this.

But the truth about the Good News is primarily this: "People, what are you waiting for? Give thanks and rejoice! Jesus Christ said, It is finished. The Good News is: that from God's viewpoint, your sins are already forgiven."

RECOMMENDED READING

On Prayer

Parker, Dr. William, & Elaine St. Johns, *Prayer Can Change Your Life* (Prentice-Hall)

Olson, Kermit, *First Steps in Prayer* (Revell)

Day, Albert E., *An Autobiography of Prayer* (Harpers)

Baille, *Diary of Private Prayer* (Scribners)

On Jesus Christ

Bickersteth, Edward, *The Trinity* (Kregel)

Simpson, P. Carnegie, *The Fact of Christ* (Clarke, London or Inter-Varsity Press)

Phillips, J. B., *Is God at Home?* (Abingdon Press)

Phillips, J. B., *When God Became Man* (Abingdon Press)

Nelson, Wesley, *Capitivated by Christ* (CLC)

Rinker, Rosalind, *Who Is This Man?* (Zondervan) A Bible study booklet for personal or group study, using the inductive study method. The contents seeks to bring the Humanity and Deity of Jesus Christ to us in much the same way as He revealed Himself when He was "in the flesh" and walking among men on earth. A natural companion piece to *Prayer—Conversing with God.*

On Quiet Time

Price, Eugenia, *Share My Pleasant Stones* (Zondervan)

Scripture Union Bible Study. Quarterly study notes published in the form of small booklets for various age groups. Samples sent on request. P.O. Box 269, Upper Darby, Pa. 19084.

Search the Scriptures (Inter-Varsity Press) Through the Bible in three years of daily readings.

HOW THIS BOOK HAS HELPED MANY

The excerpts below are from unsolicited letters of testimony to the effectiveness of this book of Prayer. These have been selected from a great number of letters received by the author.

"Rosalind Rinker's book on prayer caused me to want to learn to pray aloud."—Mrs. C.B., Kansas City, Mo.

"Now that I have read *Prayer—Conversing With God*, I have the courage and the incentive to start a small prayer

group in my own church. Until now I have been too timid."
— Miss Jane S., Charleston, W. Va.

"I have a Bible class of young housewives, and they have read *Prayer — Conversing With God* chapter by chapter. Then they split into small groups and pray conversationally. You should see them, all dressed in pedal-pushers!"— M.R., Calif.

"Our family found conversational prayer quite helpful. Like others, we fell into the rut of praying the same old thing in the same old way every evening in our family devotions. Then we began to use the Conversational Prayer approach, and a new dimension was added to our family life—we all responded, children and parents."—T. A. Bryant, Editor-in-Chief, Zondervan Publishing House.

"I am a minister's wife. My husband and I had never prayed together until we both read *Prayer—Conversing With God*."—Mrs. J.H., Bangor, Maine.

"Thank you deeply for your wonderful book. I mean it when I say it's one of the finest books I've ever read in my life. I began reading it as soon as it came. I couldn't put it down, . . . it is at the present time in the hands of a friend with whom soon I shall pray. I prayed with her over the telephone this morning. I had never done this before, and I hope God doesn't mind that I sounded more like a plumber than like an English teacher!"—B.B., Calif.

"Miss Rinker's book on *Prayer—Conversing With God* is the most revolutionary and practical method we have ever known. In our prayer groups, people are praying now who never dared say a word before. I have purchased dozens of this book and sent them far and near. We now have them for sale on a shelf in our drugstore, and the first dozen went in no time at all."—A. Ostrom, Calif.

"Miss Rinker, author of the best-seller, *Prayer—Conversing With God* tells you how personal and group praying can be exciting. You'll find yourself saying, "That's my problem!' as you read Miss Rinker's account of her own prayer difficulties as a young person. And you'll say, 'Why, this is easy!' as you read her explanation of effective group praying. Your church youth group will mean more for Christ if you read and practice the principles in this book. *This is one of the finest books on prayer for teen-agers we have ever seen!*"—*Teen-Age Book Club.*

"*Prayer—Conversing With God* is a book that is alive. It

is a book to hand to anybody who wants to know God. It is different. Its language is simple. It turns your eyes upon Jesus Christ."—M.W., Texas.

"I am absolutely convinced that God has and will bless this manner of conversational prayer. This He does, because it eliminates all stiffness and artificiality. Before I read *Prayer—Conversing With God*, I had heard about this manner of praying and wasn't sure I agreed with you. However, since reading your book my whole attitude has changed. The Lord wants us to express our love to Him, not in the lofty terms that may hinder the expression itself, but in the endearing manner of a warm love."—Lucy S. (English Professor), Tenn.

"Conversational Prayer has been put into practice in our Indian church here at Karmala, and all are desirous of keeping up this fellowship prayer. The results are heartwarming."—M. Jenkins, India.

"This is the best, direct, understandable book on Prayer I have come across. It is so simple that those who really desire to know how to pray, can, by easy steps learn. The author is most definite and most positive, as step by step she leads the reader into prayer, faith, and a realization that prayer *is* conversation with God, and that we must await His reply. The several helps for personal and group aids in prayer sum it all up, 'perfect.' This book should be used in every Young People's Group."—Mrs. G.E.D. (Southern Baptist), S.C.

"Thank you for writing—*Prayer—Conversing With God*. I have used it practically every day since I got it. You have so many wonderful ideas. At present, I am using it during the teachers and officers meeting on Wednesday nights before prayer meeting. We are discussing your book chapter by chapter."—Marie W., Bakersfield, Calif.

"Your book was given to me by a friend day before yesterday. Yesterday I was asked for the first time in my life to pray for someone's healing with a group. I was scared half to death! But I dropped everything and read *Prayer—Conversing With God*. The prayer meeting was a real living experience of the Presence of the God to whom I had just learned to pray directly—and not for the ears of those in the group."—M.H., Chicago, Ill.

"Bringing the impact of the message contained in *Prayer—Conversing With God* to Winnetka, we have successfully transformed our church staff prayer meetings, the prayer sessions of our church board, and the prayer time in our midweek service. We introduced conversational prayer into small prayer groups which were formed in our membership with a very salutary effect. Several of our people have testified to the fact that this method of praying has given their children a deeper sense of participation in family worship. I am certain that God has for this book, a very practical and far-reaching ministry."—Harold J. DeVries, Pastor, Winnetka Bible Church, Winnetka, Illinois.